Q

Queen Victoria, her girlhood and womanhood

by Grace Greenwood

PART I.

CHILDHOOD AND GIRLHOOD.

CHAPTER I.

It seems to me that the life of Queen Victoria cannot well be told without a prefacing sketch of her cousin, the Princess Charlotte, who, had she lived, would have been her Queen, and who was in many respects her prototype. It is certain, I think, that Charlotte Augusta of Wales, that lovely miracle-flower of a loveless marriage, blooming into a noble and gracious womanhood, amid the petty strifes and disgraceful intrigues of a corrupt Court, by her virtues and graces, by her high spirit and frank and fearless character, prepared the way in the loyal hearts of the British people, for the fair young kinswoman, who, twenty-one years after her own sad death, reigned in her stead.

Through all the bright life of the Princess Charlotte—from her beautiful childhood to her no less beautiful maturity—the English people had regarded her proudly and lovingly as their sovereign, who was to be; they had patience with the melancholy madness of the poor old King, her grandfather, and with the scandalous irregularities of the Prince Regent, her father, in looking forward to happier and better things under a good woman's reign; and after all those fair hopes had been coffined with her, and buried in darkness and silence, their hearts naturally turned to the royal little girl, who might possibly fill the place left so drearily vacant. England had always been happy and prosperous under Queens, and a Queen, please God, they would yet have.

The Princess Charlotte was the only child of the marriage of the Prince Regent, afterwards George IV., with the Princess Caroline of Brunswick, Her childhood was overshadowed by the hopeless estrangement of her parents. She seems to have especially loved her mother, and by the courage and independence she displayed in her championship of that good- hearted but most eccentric and imprudent woman, endeared herself to the English people, who equally admired her pluck and her filial piety—on the maternal side. They took a fond delight in relating stories of rebellion against her august papa, and even against her awful grandmamma, Queen Charlotte. They told how once, when a mere slip of a girl, being forbidden to pay her usual visit to her poor mother, she insisted on going, and on the Queen undertaking to detain her by force, resisted, struggling right valiantly, and after damaging and setting comically awry the royal mob-cap, broke away, ran out of the palace, sprang into a hackney-coach, and promising the driver a guinea, was soon at her mother's house and in her mother's arms. There is another—a Court version of this hackney-coach story—which states that it was not the Queen, but the Prince Regent that the Princess ran away from—so that there could have been no assault on a mob-cap. But the common people of that day preferred the version I have given, as more piquant, especially as old Queen Charlotte was known to be the most

3

solemnly grand of grandmammas, and a personage of such prodigious dignity that it was popularly supposed that only Kings and Queens, with their crowns actually on their heads, were permitted to sit in her presence.

As a young girl, the Princess Charlotte was by no means without faults of temper and manner. She was at times self-willed, passionate, capricious, and imperious, though ordinarily good-humored, kindly, and sympathetic. A Court lady of the time, speaking of her, says: "She is very clever, but at present has the manners of a hoyden school-girl. She talked all sorts of nonsense to me, but can put on dignity when she chooses." This writer also relates that the royal little lady loved to shock her attendants by running to fetch for herself articles she required—her hat, a book, or a chair—and that one summer, when she stayed at a country-house, she would even run to open the gate to visitors, curtsying to them like a country lassie. The Earl of Albemarle, who was her playmate in childhood, his grandmother being her governess, relates that one time when they had the Prince Regent to lunch, the chop came up spoiled, and it was found that Her Royal Highness had descended into the kitchen, and, to the dismay of the cook, insisted on broiling it. Albemarle adds that he, boy-like, taunted her with her culinary failure, saying: "*You* would make a pretty Queen, wouldn't you?" At another time, some years later, she came in her carriage to make a morning-call at his grandmother's, and seeing a crowd gathered before the door, attracted by the royal liveries, she ran out a back-way, came round, and mingled with the curious throng unrecognized, and as eager to see the Princess as any of them.

Not being allowed the society of her mother, and that of her father not being considered wholesome for her, the Princess was early advised and urged to take a companion and counsellor in the shape of a husband. The Prince of Orange, afterwards King of the Netherlands, was fixed upon as a good *parti* by her royal relatives, and he came courting to the English Court. But the Princess did hot altogether fancy this aspirant, so, after her independent fashion, she declined the alliance, and "the young man went away sorrowing."

One of the ladies of the Princess used to tell how for a few minutes after the Prince had called to make his sad *adieux*, she hoped that Her Royal Highness had relented because she walked thoughtfully to the window to see the last of him as he descended the palace steps and sprang into his carriage, looking very grand in his red uniform, with a tuft of green feathers in his hat. But when the Princess turned away with a gay laugh, saying, "How like a radish he looks," she knew that all was over. It is an odd little coincidence, that a later Prince of Orange, afterwards King of the Netherlands, had the same bad luck as a suitor to the Princess or Queen Victoria.

Charlotte's next lover, Leopold, of Saxe-Coburg, an amiable and able Prince, was more fortunate. He won the light but constant heart of the Princess, inspiring her not only with tender love, but with profound respect. Her high spirit and imperious will were soon tamed to his firm but gentle hand; she herself became more gentle and reasonable, content to rule the kingdom of his heart at least, by her womanly charms, rather than by the power of her regal name and lofty position. This royal love-marriage took place in May, 1816, and soon after the Prince and Princess, who had little taste for Court gaieties, went to live at Claremont, the beautiful country residence now occupied by the young Duke of Albany, a namesake of Prince Leopold. Here the young couple lived a life of much domestic privacy and simplicity, practicing themselves in habits of study, methodical application to business, and wise economy. They were always together, spending happy hours in work and recreation, passing from law and politics to music and sketching, from the study of the British Constitution to horticulture. The Princess especially delighted in gardening, in watering with her own hands her favorite plants.

4

This happy pair had an invaluable aid and ally in the learned Baron Stockmar, early attached to Prince Leopold as private physician, a rare, good man on whom they both leaned much, as afterwards did Victoria and Albert and their children. Indeed the Baron seems to have been a permanent pillar for princes to lean upon. From youth to old age he was to two or three royal households the chief "guide, philosopher, and friend"—a Coburg mentor, a Guelphic oracle.

So these royal lovers of Claremont lived tranquilly on, winning the love and respect of all about them, and growing dearer and dearer to each other till the end came, the sudden death of the young wife and mother,— an event which, on a sad day in November, 1817, plunged the whole realm into mourning. The grief of the people, even those farthest removed from the Court, was real, intense, almost personal and passionate. It was a double tragedy, for the child too was dead. The accounts of the last moments of the Princess are exceedingly touching. When told that her baby boy was not living, she said: "I am grieved, for myself, for the English people, but O, above all, I feel it for my dear husband!" Taking an opportunity when the Prince was away from her bedside, she asked if she too must die. The physician did not directly reply, but said, "Pray be calm."

"I know what *that* means," she replied, then added, "Tell it to my husband,—tell it with caution and tenderness, and be sure to say to him, from me, that I am still the happiest wife in England."

It seems, according to the Queen, that it was Stockmar that took this last message to the Prince, who lacked the fortitude to remain by the bedside of his dying wife—that it was Stockmar who held her hand till it grew pulseless and cold, till the light faded from her sweet blue eyes as her great life and her great love passed forever from the earth. Yet it seems that through a mystery of transmigration, that light and life and love were destined soon to be reincarnated in a baby cousin, born in May, 1819, called at first "the little May-flower," and through her earliest years watched and tended as a frail and delicate blossom of hope.

CHAPTER II.

Birth of the Princess Victoria—Character of her Father—Question of the Succession to the Throne—Death of the Duke of Kent—Baptism of Victoria —Removal to Woolbrook Glen—Her first Escape from Sudden Death—Picture of Domestic Life—Anecdotes.

After the loss of his wife, Prince Leopold left for a time his sad home of Claremont, and returned to the Continent, but came back some time in 1819, to visit a beloved sister, married since his own bereavement, and become the mother of a little English girl, and for the second time a widow. Lovingly, though with a pang at his heart, the Prince bent over the cradle of this eight-months-old baby, who in her unconscious orphanage smiled into his kindly face, and though he thought sorrowfully of the little one whose eyes had never smiled into his, had never even opened upon life, he vowed then and there to the child of his bereaved sister, the devoted love, the help, sympathy, and guidance which never failed her while he lived.

This baby girl was the daughter of the Duke of Kent and of the Princess Victoire Marie Louise of Saxe-Coburg Saalfield, widow of Prince Charles of Leiningen. Edward, Duke of Kent, was the fourth and altogether the best son of George III. Making all allowance for the exaggeration of loyal biographers, I should say he was an amiable, able, and upright man, generous and charitable to a remarkable degree, for a royal Prince of that time—perhaps too much so, for he kept himself poor and died poor. He was not a favorite with his royal parents, who seem to have denied him reasonable assistance, while lavishing large sums on his spendthrift brother, the Prince of Wales. George was like the prodigal son of Scripture, except that he never repented—Edward like the virtuous son, except that he never complained.

On the death of the Princess Charlotte the Duke of York had become heir- presumptive to the throne. He had no children, and the Duke of Clarence, third son of George III., was therefore next in succession. He married in the same year as his brother of Kent, and to him also a little daughter was born, who, had she lived, would have finally succeeded to the throne instead of Victoria. But the poor little Princess stayed but a little while to flatter or disappoint royal hopes. She looked timidly out upon life, with all its regal possibilities, and went away untempted. Still the Duchess of Clarence (afterwards Queen Adelaide) might yet be the happy mother of a Prince, or Princess Royal, and there were so many probabilities against the accession of the Duke of Kent's baby to the throne that people smiled when, holding her in his arms, the proud father would say, in a spirit of prophecy, "Look at her well!—she will yet be Queen of England."

One rainy afternoon the Duke stayed out late, walking in the grounds, and came in with wet feet. He was urged to change his boots and stockings, but his pretty baby, laughing and crowing on her mother's knee, was too much for him; he took her in his arms and played with her till the fatal chill struck him. He soon took to his bed, which he never left. He had inflammation of the lungs, and a country doctor, which last took from him one hundred and twenty ounces of blood. Then, as he grew no better, a great London physician was called in, but he said it was too late to save the illustrious patient; that if he had had charge of the case at first, he would have "bled more freely." Such was the medical system of sixty years ago.

The Duke of Kent's death brought his unconscious baby's feet a step—just his grave's width—nearer the throne; but it was not till many years later—till after the death of her kindly uncle of York, and her "fine gentleman" uncle, George IV., and the accession of her rough sailor- uncle, the Duke of Clarence, William IV., an old man, and legally considered childless—that the Princess Victoria was confidently regarded as the coming sovereign, and that the momentous truth was revealed to her. She was twelve years old before any clear intimation had been allowed to reach her of the exceptional grandeur of her destiny. Till then she did not know that she was especially an object of national love and hope, or especially great or fortunate. She knew that she was a "Royal Highness," but she knew also, the wise child!—that since the Guelphs came over to rule the English, Royal Highnesses had been more plentiful than popular; she knew that she was obliged to wear, most of the time, very plain cotton gowns and straw hats, and to learn a lot of tiresome things, and that she was kept on short allowance of pin-money and ponies.

The wise Duchess of Kent certainly guarded her with the most jealous care from all premature realization of the splendid part she might have to play in the world's history, as a hope too intoxicating, or a responsibility too heavy, for the heart and mind of a sensitive child.

I wonder if her Serene Highness kept fond motherly records of the babyhood and childhood of the Queen? If so, what a rich mine it would be for a poor bewildered biographer like me, required to make my foundation bricks with only a few golden bits of straw. I have searched the chronicles of the writers of that time; I have questioned loyal old people, but have found or gained little that is novel, or peculiarly interesting.

Victoria was born in the sombre but picturesque old palace of Kensington, on May 24, 1819, and on the 24th of the following June was baptized with great pomp out of the splendid gold font, brought from the Tower, by the Archbishop of Canterbury, assisted by the Bishop of London. Her sponsors were the Prince Regent and the Emperor of Russia (the last represented by the Duke of York), the Queen Dowager of Würtemburg (represented by the Princess Augusta) and the Duchess Dowager of Coburg (represented by the Duchess Dowager of Gloucester), and her names were *Alexandrina Victoria*, the first in honor of the Emperor Alexander of Russia. She came awfully near being Alexandrina Georgiana, but the Prince Regent, at the last moment, declared that the name of Georgiana should be second to no other; then added, "Give her her mother's name—after that of the Emperor." The Queen afterwards decided that her mother's name should be second to no other. Yet as a child she was often called "little Drina."

The baby's first move from her stately birthplace was to a lovely country residence called Woolbrook Glen, near Sidmouth. Here Victoria had the first of those remarkable narrow escapes from sudden and violent death which have almost seemed to prove that she bears a "charmed life." A boy was shooting sparrows in vicinity of the house, and a charge from his carelessly-handled gun pierced the window by which the nurse was sitting, with the little Princess in her arms. It is stated that the shot passed frightfully near the head of the child. But she was as happily unconscious of the deadly peril she had been in as, a few months later, she was of the sad loss she sustained in the death of her father, who was laid away with the other Guelphs in the Windsor Royal Vault, never again to throne his little "Queen" in his loyal, loving arms.

The Princess Victoria seems to have been always ready for play, dearly loving a romp. One of the earliest mentions I find of her is in the correspondence of Bishop Wilberforce. After stating that he had been summoned to the presence of the Duchess of Kent, he says: "She received me with her fine, animated child on the floor by her side busy with its playthings, of which I soon became one."

This little domestic picture gives a glimpse of the tender intimacy, the constant companionship of this noble mother with her child. It is stated that, unlike most mothers in high life, the Duchess nursed this illustrious child at her own breast, and so mingled her life with its life that nothing thenceforth could divide them. The wee Princess passed happily through the perils of infantile ailments. She cut her teeth as easily as most children, with the help of her gold-mounted coral—and very nice teeth they were, though a little too prominent according to the early pictures. If the infant Prince Albert reminded his grandmamma of a "weasel," his "pretty cousin" might have suggested to her a squirrel by "a little something about the mouth."

An old newspaper writer gave a rather rapturous and pompous account of the Princess Victoria when she was about three years old. He says: "Passing through Kensington Gardens a few days since, I observed at some distance a party consisting of several ladies, a young child, and two men-servants, having in charge a donkey, gayly caparisoned with blue ribbons, and accoutred for the use of the infant." He soon ascertained that the party was the Duchess of Kent and her daughter, the Princess Feodore of Leiningen, and the Princess Alexandrina Victoria. On his approaching them the little one replied to his "respectful recognition" with a pleasant "good-morning," and he noted that she was equally polite to all who politely greeted her—truly one "to the manner born." This writer adds: "Her Royal Highness is remarkably beautiful, and her gay and animated countenance bespeaks perfect health and good temper. Her complexion is excessively fair, her eyes large and expressive, and her cheeks blooming. She bears a striking resemblance to her royal father."

A glimpse which Leigh Hunt gives of his little liege lady, as she appeared to him for the first time in Kensington Gardens, is interesting, as revealing the child's affectionate disposition. "She was coming up a cross-path from the Bayswater Gate, with a little girl of her own age by her side, whose hand she was holding as though she loved her." And why not, Mr. Poet? Princesses, especially Princesses of the bread-and-butter age, are as susceptible to joys of sympathy and companionship as any of us—untitled poets and title-contemning Republicans.

Lord Albemarle, in his autobiography, speaks of watching, in an idle hour, from the windows of the old palace, "the movements of a bright, pretty little girl, seven years of age, engaged in watering the plants immediately under the window. It was amusing to see how impartially she divided the contents of the watering-pot between the flowers and her own little feet. Her simple but becoming dress—a large straw hat and a white cotton gown—contrasted favorably with the gorgeous apparel now worn by the little damsels of the rising generation. A colored fichu round the neck was the only ornament she wore. The young lady I am describing was the Princess Victoria, now our Gracious Sovereign."

Queen Victoria dressed her own children in the same simple style, voted quaint and old-fashioned by a later generation. I heard long ago a story of a fashionable lady from some provincial town taking a morning walk in Windsor Park, in the wild hope of a glimpse of royalty, and meeting a lady and gentleman, accompanied only by two or three children, and all so plainly dressed that she merely glanced at them as they passed. Some distance further she walked in her eager quest, when she met an old Scotch gardener, of whom she asked if there was any chance of her encountering the Queen anywhere on the domain. "Weel, ye maun, turn back and rin a good bit, for you've passed her *Mawjesty*, the Prince, and the Royal bairns."

Ah, wasn't she spited as she looked back and saw the joyous family party in the dim distance, and realized what she had lost in not indulging herself in a good long British stare, and what a sin she had committed in not making a loyal British obeisance.

CHAPTER III.

Victoria's early Education—Anecdote—Routine of Life at Kensington Palace—Character and Circumstances of the Duchess of Kent—Anecdote—Simple Mode of Life—Visits.

Queen Victoria tells little of her childhood, but speaks of it as rather "dull." It seems, however, to have never been empty or idle. All her moments were golden—for study, or for work, or healthful exercise and play. She was taught, and perhaps was inclined, to waste no time, and to be careful not to cause others to waste it. A dear English friend contributes the following anecdote, slight, but very significant, obtained long ago from a lady whose young daughters, then at school at Hammersmith, had the same writing-master as the Princess Victoria: "Of course," says my friend, "every incident connected with the little Princess was interesting to the school-girls, and all that this master (I think his name was Steward) had to tell went to prove her a kind-hearted and considerate child.

"She always mentioned to him in advance the days on which she would not require a lesson, saying: 'I thought, perhaps, you would like to know.' Sometimes she would say, 'We are going to Windsor to see Uncle King,' or she would name some other important engagement. By 'Uncle King' she meant George IV. Mr. Steward, of course, availed himself of the liberty suggested by the little Princess, then about eight years old, by whose thoughtful kindness he was saved much time and trouble."

Lord Campbell, speaking of the Princess as a little girl, says: "She seems in good health, and appears lively and good-humored." It may be that the good-humor was, in great part, the result of the good health.

The Princess was brought up after the wisest, because most simple, system of healthful living: perfect regularity in the hours of eating, sleeping, and exercise; much life in the open air, and the least possible excitement.

She was taught to respect her own constitution as well as that of the British Government, and to reverence the laws of health as the laws of God.

An account which I judge to be authoritative of the daily routine of the family life in Kensington, runs thus: "Breakfast at 8 o'clock in summer, the Princess Victoria having her bread and milk and fruit put on a little table by her mother's side. After breakfast the Princess Feodore studied with her governess, and the Princess Victoria went out for an

8

hour's walk or drive. From 10 to 12 her mother instructed her, after which she could amuse herself by running through the suite of rooms which extended round two sides of the palace, and in which were many of her toys. At 2 a plain dinner, while her mother took her luncheon. Lessons again till 4; then would come a visit or drive, and after that a walk or donkey ride in the gardens. At the time of her mother's dinner the Princess had her supper, still at the side of the Duchess; then, after playing with her nurse (Mrs. Brock, whom she called 'dear, dear Boppy'), she would join the party at dessert, and at 9 she would retire to her bed, which was placed at the side of her mother's."

We see regular study, regular exercise, simple food, plenty of outdoor air, plenty of play, plenty of sleep. It seems that when this admirable mother laid her child away from her own breast, it was only to lay it on that of Nature, and very close has Victoria, with all her state and grandeur, kept to the heart of the great all-mother ever since.

The Duchess of Kent was left not only with very limited means for a lady of her station, but also burdened by her husband's debts, which, being a woman with a fine sense of honor, she felt herself obliged to discharge, or at least to reduce as far and fast as possible. Had it not been for help from her generous brother, Leopold, she could hardly have afforded for her daughter the full and fitting education she received. So, had not her taste and her sense of duty towards her child inclined her to a life of quiet and retirement, the lack of fortune would have constrained her to live simply and modestly. As it was, privacy was the rule in the life of the accomplished Duchess, still young and beautiful, and in that of her little shadow; very seldom did they appear at Court, or in any gay Court circle; so, at the time of her accession to the throne, Victoria might almost have been a fairy-princess, emerging from some enchanted dell in Windsor forest, or a water-nymph evoked from the Serpentine in Kensington Gardens by some modern Merlin, for all the world at large—the world beyond her kingdom at least—knew of her young years, of her character and disposition. Now few witnesses are left anywhere of her fair happy childhood, or even of her girlhood, which was like a silvery crescent, holding the dim promise of full-orbed womanhood and Queenhood.

As the Princess grew older, she found loving and helpful companionship in her half-brother and sister, Prince Charles and the Princess Feodore of Leiningen, the three children and their mother forming a close family union, which years and separations and changes of fortune never destroyed. They are all gone from her now; the Queen, as daughter and sister, stands alone.

A kind friend and a well-known English writer, F. Aiken Kortright, for many years a resident of Kensington, tells some pleasant little local stories of the Princess Victoria. She says: "In her childhood the Princess Victoria was frequently seen in a little carriage, drawn over the gravel-walks of the then rural Kensington Gardens, accompanied by her elder and half-sister, the Princess Feodore, and attended by a single servant. Many elderly people still remember the extreme simplicity of the child's attire, and the quiet and unpretentious appearance and manners of her sister, who was one day seen to stop the tiny carriage to indulge the fancy of an unknown little girl by allowing her to kiss her future Queen."

That "unknown little girl" was an elder sister of Miss Kortright. My friend also says that the Duchess of Kent and her daughters frequently on summer afternoons took tea on the lawn, "in sight of admiring promenaders, with a degree of publicity which now sounds fabulous."

It was then safe and agreeable for that quiet, refined family, only because the London "Rough"—that ugly, unwholesome, fungous growth on the fine old oak of English character—had not made his unwelcome appearance in all the public parks of the metropolis. Our friend also states that so simple and little-girlish was the Princess in her ways that, later on, she was known to go with her mother or sister to a Kensington

9

milliner's to buy a hat, stay to have it trimmed, and then carry it (or more likely the old one) home in her hand. I should like to see a little Miss Vanderbilt do a thing of that kind!

The Kents and Leiningens—if I may speak so familiarly of Royal and Serene Highnesses—when away from the quiet home in Kensington, spent much time at lovely Claremont as guests of the dear brother and Uncle Leopold. They seem also to have travelled a good deal in England, visiting watering-places and in houses of the nobility, but never to have gone over to the Continent. The Duchess probably felt that the precious life which she held in trust for the people of England might possibly be endangered by too long journeys, or by changes of climate; but what it cost to the true German woman to so long exile herself from her old home and her kindred none ever knew—at least none among her husband's unsympathetic family—for she was, as a Princess, too proud to complain; as a mother, cheerful in her devotion and self-abnegation.

CHAPTER IV.

Queen-making not a Light Task—Admirable Discipline of the Duchess of Kent—Foundation of the Character and Habits of the future Queen—Curious Extract from a Letter by her Grandmamma—A Children's Ball given by George IV. to the little Queen of Portugal—A Funny Mishap—Death of George IV.—Character of his Successor—Victoria's first appearance at a Drawing-room—Her absence from the Coronation of William IV.

Queen-making is not a light task. It is no fancywork for idle hours. It is the first difficult draft of a chapter, perhaps a whole volume, of national history.

No woman ever undertook a more important labor than did the widowed Duchess of Kent, or carried it out with more faithfulness, if we may judge by results.

The lack of fortune in the family was not an unmixed evil; perhaps it was even one of those disagreeable "blessings in disguise," which nobody welcomes, but which the wise profit by, as it caused the Duchess to impress upon her children, especially the child Victoria, the necessity of economy, and the safety and dignity which one always finds in living within one's income. Frugality, exactitude in business, faithfulness to all engagements, great or small, punctuality, that economy of time, are usually set down among the minor moralities of life, more humdrum than heroic; but under how many circumstances and conditions do they reveal themselves as cardinal virtues, as things on which depend the comfort and dignity of life! It seems that these things were so impressed on the mind and heart of the young Victoria by her careful, methodical German mother, that they became a part of her conscience, entered so deeply into the rule of her life that no after-condition of wealth, or luxury, or sovereign independence; no natural desire for ease or pleasure; no passion of love or grief; no possible exigencies of imperial state have been able to overcome or set them aside. The danger is that such rigid principles, such systematic habits, adopted in youth, may in age become, from being the ministers of one's will, the tyrants of one's life.

It seems to be somewhat so in the case of the Queen, for I hear it said that the sun, the moon, and the tides are scarcely more punctual and regular in their rounds and mighty offices, in their coming and going, than she in the daily routine of her domestic and state duties and frequent journeyings; and that the laws of the Medes and Persians are as naught in inexorableness and inflexibility to the rules and regulations of Windsor and Balmoral.

But the English people, even those directly inconvenienced at times by those unbending habits and irrevocable rules, have no right to find fault, for these be the right royal results of the admirable but somewhat unyouthful qualities they adored in the young Queen. They have no right to sneer because a place of honor is given in Her Majesty's household to that meddlesome, old-fashioned German country cousin, Economy; for did not they all rejoice in the early years of the reign to hear of this same dame being introduced by those clever managers, Prince Albert and Baron Stockmar, into the royal palaces, wherein she had not been seen for many a year?

But to return to the little Princess. The Duchess, her mother, seems to have given her all needful change of air and scene, though always maintaining; habits of study, and an admirable system of mental and moral training; for the child's constitution seems to have strengthened year by year, and in spite of one or two serious attacks of illness, the foundation was laid of the robust health which, accompanied by rare courage and nerve, has since so marked and blessed her life. A writer of the time speaks of a visit paid by her and her mother to Windsor in 1829, when the child was about seven years old, and states that George IV., her "Uncle King," was delighted with her "charming manners."

It was about this visit that her maternal grandmamma at Coburg wrote to her mamma: "I see by the English papers that Her Royal Highness the Duchess of Kent went on Virginia water with His Majesty. The little monkey must have pleased and amused him, she is such a pretty, clever child."

To think of the great Victoria, Queen of Great Britain and Ireland, and Empress of India, being called "a little monkey"! Grandmammas will take such liberties. Three or four years later, according to that spicy and irreverent chronicler, Charles Greville, the little Princess was not pretty. But she was just entering on that ungracious period in which few little girls are comely to look upon, or comfortable to themselves. Greville saw her at a children's ball, given by the King in honor of his little guest, the child-Queen of Portugal, Donna Maria II., da Gloria, whom the King seated at his right hand, and was very attentive to. Greville says she was fine-looking and very finely dressed, "with a ribbon and order over her shoulder," and she must have seemed very grand to the other children while she sat by the King, but when she came to dance she "fell down and hurt her face, was frightened and bruised, and went away." Then he adds: "Our little Princess is a short, plain child, not so good-looking as the Portuguese. However, if Nature has not done so much, Fortune is likely to do a great deal more for her."

Victoria did not know that, but like any other little girl she may, perhaps, have comforted herself by thinking, "Well, if I'm not so handsome and grand and smartly dressed as that Maria, I'm less awkward. I was able to keep my head and not lose my feet."

As for her small Majesty of Portugal, she was at that time a Queen without a crown and without a kingdom. She had come all the way from Brazil to take her grandfather's throne, a little present from her father, Dom Pedro I., the rightful heir, but only to find the place filled by a wicked uncle, Don Miguel. She had a long fight with the usurper, her father coming over to help her, and finally ousted Miguel and got into that big, uneasy arm-chair, called a throne, where she continued to sit, though much shaken and heaved up and about by political convulsions, for some dozen years, when she found it best to step down and out.

It is said she did not gain, but lost in beauty as she grew to womanhood; so finally the English Princess had the advantage of her in the matter of good looks even.

King George IV., though he was fond of his amusing little niece, did not like to think of her as destined to rule in his place. He is said to have been much offended when, as he was proposing to give that ball, his chief favorite, a gay, Court lady, exclaimed: "Oh, do! it will be so nice to see the *two little Queens* dancing together." Yet he disliked the Duchess of Kent for keeping the child as much as possible away from his disreputable Court, and educating her after her own ideas, and often threatened to use his power as King to deprive her of the little girl. The country would not have stood this, yet the Duchess must have suffered cruelly from fear of having her darling child taken from her by this crowned ogre, and shut up in the gloomy keep of his Castle at Windsor. But it was the Ogre-King who was taken, a little more than a year after the children's ball—and not a day too soon for his country's good—and his brother, the Duke of Clarence, reigned in his stead.

William IV. had some heart, some frankness and honesty, but he was a bluff, rough sailor, and when excited, oaths of the hottest sort flew from his lips, like sparks from an anvil. Because of his roughness and profanity, and because, perhaps, of the fact of his surrounding himself with a lot of natural children, the Duchess was determined to persevere in her retirement from the Court circle, and in keeping her innocent little daughter out of its unwholesome atmosphere, as much as possible. She was, however, most friendly with Queen Adelaide, who, when her last child died, had written to her: "My children are dead, but yours lives, and she is mine too." The good woman meant this, and her fondness was returned by Victoria, who manifested for her to the last, filial affection and consideration.

The first Drawing-room which the Princess attended was one given in honor of Her Majesty's birthday. She went with her mother and a suite of ladies and gentlemen in State carriages, escorted by a party of Life Guards. The Princess was on that occasion dressed entirely in materials of British manufacture, her frock being of English blonde, very simple and becoming. She stood at the left of her aunt, the Queen, and watched the splendid ceremony with great interest, while everybody watched her with greater interest. But if the presence of the "heir-presumptive to the throne" created a sensation at the Queen's Drawing-room, her absence from the King's coronation created more. Some said it was because a proper place in the procession—one next to the King and Queen—had not been assigned to her; others, that the Duchess had kept her away on account of her delicate health, and nobody knew exactly the truth of the matter. Perhaps the great state secret will be revealed some day with the identity of "Junius" and the "Man in the Iron Mask."

CHAPTER V.

King William jealous of Public Honors to Victoria—Anecdote—The unusual Studies of the Princess—Her Visits to the Isle of Wight—Laughable Incident at Wentworth House—Anecdote related by her Music-teacher— Unwholesome adulation of the Princess—Reflections upon the curious isolation of her Social Position—Extract from one of her later Letters.

The indifference of the Duchess of Kent to the heavy pomps and heavier gayeties of his Court so offended his unmajestic Majesty, that he finally became decidedly inimical to the Duchess. Though he insisted on seeing the little Princess often, he did not like the English people to see too much of her, or to pay her and her mother too much honor. He objected to their little journeys, calling them "royal progresses," and by a special order put a stop to the "poppings," in the way of salutes, to the vessel which bore them to and from the Isle of Wight—a small piece of state- business for a King and his Council to be engaged in. The King's unpopular brother, the Duke of Cumberland, was also supposed to be unfriendly to the widow of a brother whom he had not loved, and to the child whom, according to that brother, he regarded from the first as an "intruder," and who certainly at the last, stood between His Royal Grossness and the throne—the throne which would have gone down under him. Yet, in spite of enmity and opposition from high quarters, and jealousy and harsh criticism from Court ministers and minions, the Duchess of Kent, who seems to have been a woman of immense firmness and resolution, kept on her way, rearing her daughter as she thought best, coming and going as she felt inclined.

Victoria's governess was for many years the accomplished Baroness Lehzen, who had also been the chief instructress of her sister, Feodore. Until she was twelve years old, her masters were also German, and she is said to have spoken English with a German accent. After that time her teachers, in nearly all branches, were English. Miss Kortright tells me a little anecdote of the Princess when about twelve years old, related by one of these teachers. She had been reading in her classical history the story of Cornelia, the mother of the Gracchi—how she proudly presented her sons to the ostentatious and much-bediamonded Roman dame, with the words, "These are *my* jewels." "She should have said my *Cornelians*," said the quick-witted little girl.

Victoria was instructed in some things not in those days thought proper for young ladies to learn, but deemed necessary for a poor girl who was expected to do a man's work. She was well grounded in history, instructed in Latin—though she did not fancy it, and later, in the British Constitution, and in law and politics. Nor were light accomplishments neglected: in modern languages, in painting and music, she finally became singularly proficient. Gifted with a remarkably sweet voice and a correct ear, she could not well help being a charming singer, under her great master, Lablache. She danced well, rode well, and excelled in archery.

As I said, the brave Duchess, as conscientious as independent, kept up the life of retirement from Court pomps and gayeties, and of alternate hard study and social recreation, which she thought best for her child.

She quietly persevered in the "progresses" which annoyed the irascible and unreasonable old King, even visiting the Isle of Wight, though the royal big guns were forbidden to "pop" at sight of the royal standard, which waved over her, and the young hope of England. Perhaps recollections of those pleasant visits with her mother at Norris Castle have helped to render so dear the Queen's own beautiful sea-side home, Osborne House. I remember a pretty little story, told by a tourist, who happened to be stopping at the village of Brading during one of those visits to the lovely island. One afternoon he strolled into the old church-yard to search out the grave of Elizabeth Wallbridge, the sweet heroine of Leigh Richmond's beautiful religious story, "The Dairyman's Daughter." He found seated beside the mound a lady and a young girl, the latter reading aloud, in a full, melodious voice, the touching tale of the Christian maiden. The tourist turned away, and soon after was told by the sexton that those pilgrims to that humble grave were the Duchess of Kent and the Princess Victoria.

I am told by a Yorkshire lady another story of the Princess, of not quite so serious a character. She was visiting with her mother, of course, at Wentworth House, the seat of Earl Fitzwilliam in Yorkshire, and while at that pleasant place delighted in running about by herself in the gardens and shrubberies. One wet morning, soon after her arrival, she was thus disporting herself, flitting from point to point, light-hearted and light-footed, when the old gardener, who did not then know her, seeing her about to descend a treacherous bit of ground from the terrace, called out, "Be careful, Miss; it's slape!"—a Yorkshire word for slippery. The incautious, but ever-curious Princess, turning her head, asked, "What's slape?" and the same instant her feet flew from under her, and she came down. The old gardener ran to lift her, saying, as he did so, "*That's* slape, Miss."

There is nothing remarkable, much less incredible, in these stories of the young Victoria, nor in the one related by her music-teacher, of how she once rebelled against so much practice, and how, on his telling her that there was no "royal road" in art, and that only by much practice could she become "mistress of the piano," she closed and locked the obnoxious instrument and put the key in her pocket, saying playfully, "Now you see there *is* a royal way of becoming 'mistress of the piano.'" But not so simple and natural and girlish are all the things told of the Queen's young days. Loyal English people have

13

said to me, "You will find few stories of Her Majesty's childhood, but those few will all be good."

Yes, too good. The chroniclers of forty and fifty years ago—the same in whose loyal eyes the fifteen children of George III. were all "children of light"—could find no words in which to paint their worship for this rising star of sovereignty. According to them, she was not only the pearl of Princesses for piety and propriety, for goodness and graciousness, but a marvel of unchildlike wisdom, a prodigy of cleverness and learning; in short, a purely perfect creature, loved of the angels to a degree perilous to the succession. The simplest little events of her daily life were twisted into something unnaturally significant, or unhealthily virtuous. If she was taken through a cotton-mill at Manchester, and asked a score or two of questions about the machinery and the strange processes of spinning and weaving, it was not childish curiosity—it was a love of knowledge, and a patriotic desire to encourage British manufactures.

If she gave a few pennies to a blind beggar at Margate, the amiable act was heralded as one, of almost divine beneficence, and the beggar pitied, as never before, for his blindness. The poor man had not beheld the face of the "little angel" who dropped the coin into his greasy hat! If, full of "high spirits," she took long rides on a donkey at Ramsgate, and ran races with other children on the sands, it was a proof of the sweetest human condescension—the donkey's opinion not being taken.

Of course all this is false, unwholesome sentiment, quite incomprehensible to nineteenth century Americans, though our great- grandfathers understood this sort of personal loyalty very well, and gloried in it, till George the Third drove them to the wall; and our great-grandmothers cherished it as a sacred religious principle till their tea was taxed. I dare say that if the truth could be got at, we should find that little Victoria was at times trying enough to mother, masters, and attendants; that she was occasionally passionate, perverse, and "pestering," like all children who have any great and positive elements in them. I dare say she was disposed, like any other "only child," to be self-willed and selfish, and that she required a fair amount of wholesome discipline, and that she got it. Had she been the prim and pious little precocity which some biographers have painted her, she would have died young, like the "Dairyman's Daughter"; we might have had an edifying tract, and England a revolution.

One of her biographers speaks with a sort of ecstatic surprise of the fact that the Princess was "affable—even gay," and that she "laughed and chatted like other little girls." And yet she must early have perceived that she was not quite like other little girls, but set up and apart. Though reared with all the simplicity practicable for a Princess Royal, she must have been conscious of a magic circle drawn round her, of a barrier impalpable, but most real, which other children could not voluntarily overpass. She must have seen that they could not call out to her to "come and play!" that however shy she might feel, she must propose the game, or the romp, as later she had to propose marriage. She even was obliged to quarrel, if quarrel she did, all alone by herself. Any resistance on the part of her playmates would have been a small variety of high treason. She must sometimes, with her admirable good sense, have been wearied and disgusted by so much concession, conciliation, and consideration, and may have envied less fortunate or unfortunate mortals who can give and take hard knocks, for whom less is demanded, and of whom less is expected.

She may have tired of her very name, with its grand prefixes and no affix, and longed to be Victoria Kent, or *Something*—Jones, Brown, or Robinson.

She seems to have been a child of simple, homely tastes, for in 1842, when Queen, she writes to her Uncle Leopold from Claremont, where she is visiting, with her husband and little daughter: "This place brings back recollections of the happiest days of my otherwise dull childhood—days when I experienced such kindness from you, dearest uncle;

Victoria plays with my old bricks, and I see her running and jumping in the flower-garden, as old (though I feel still *little*) Victoria of former days used to do."

CHAPTER VI.

The Princess opens the Victoria Park at Bath—Becoming used to Public Curiosity—Secret of her Destiny revealed to her—Royal Ball on her Thirteenth Birthday—At the Ascot Races—Picture by N. P. Willis—Anecdotes—Painful Scene at the King's last Birthday Dinner.

When she was eleven years old, the Princess opened the Victoria Park at Bath. She began the opening business thus early, and has kept it up pretty diligently for fifty years—parks, expositions, colleges, exchanges, law courts, bridges, docks, art schools, and hospitals. Her sons and daughters are also kept busy at the same sort of work. Indeed these are almost the only openings for young men of the royal family for active service, now that crusades and invasions of France have gone out of fashion. It seems to me that the English people get up all sorts of opening and unveiling occasions in order to supply employment to their Princes and Princesses, who, I must say, never shirk such monotonous duties, however much they may be bothered and bored by them.

Occasionally the Duchess of Kent and her daughter visited Brighton, and stopped in that grotesque palace of George IV., called the Pavilion. I have seen a picture of the demure little Princess, walking on the esplanade, with her mother, governesses, and gentlemen attendants, the whole elegant party and the great crowd of Brightonians following and staring at them, wearing the absurd costumes of half a century ago—the ladies, big bonnets, big mutton-leg sleeves, big collars, heelless slippers, laced over the instep; the gentlemen, short-waisted coats, enormous collars, preposterous neckties, and indescribably clumsy hats.

By this time the Princess had learned to bear quietly and serenely, if not unconsciously, the gaze of hundreds of eyes, admiring or criticising. She knew that the time was probably coming when the hundreds would increase to thousands, and even millions—when the world would for her seem to be made up of eyes, like a peacock's tail. Small wonder that in her later years, especially since she has missed from her side the splendid figure which divided and justified the mighty multitudinous stare, this eternal observation, this insatiable curiosity has become infinitely wearisome to her.

Several accounts have been given of the manner in which the great secret of her destiny was revealed to the Princess Victoria, and the manner in which it was received, but only one has the Queen's indorsement. This was contained in a letter, written long afterwards to Her Majesty by her dear old governess, the Baroness Lehzen, who states that when the Regency Bill (an act naming the Duchess of Kent as Regent, in case of the King dying before his niece obtained her majority) was before Parliament, it was thought that the time had come to make known to the Princess her true position. So after consulting with the Duchess, the Baroness placed a genealogical table in a historical book, which her pupil was reading. When the Princess came upon this paper, she said: "Why, I never saw that before." "It was not thought necessary you should see it," the Baroness replied. Then the young girl, examining the paper, said thoughtfully: "I see I am nearer the throne than I supposed." After some moments she resumed, with a sort of quaint solemnity: "Now many a child would boast, not knowing the difficulty. There is much splendor, but there is also much responsibility." "The Princess," says the Baroness, "having lifted up the forefinger of her right hand while she spoke, now gave me that little hand, saying: 'I will be good. I understand now why you urged me so much to learn, even Latin. My aunts, Augusta and Mary, never did, but you told me Latin was the foundation of English grammar, and all the elegant expressions, and I learned it, as you wished it; but I understand all better now,' and the Princess again gave me her hand, repeating, 'I will be good.'"

God heard the promise of the child of twelve years and held her to it, and has given her strength "as her day" to redeem it, all through the dazzling brightness and the depressing shadows, through the glory and the sorrow of her life, as a Queen and a woman.

The Queen says that she "cried much" over the magnificent but difficult problem of her destiny, but the tears must have been April showers, for in those days she was accounted a bright, care-free little damsel, and was ever welcome as a sunbeam in the noblest houses of England—such as Eaton Hall, the seat of the Duke of Westminster; Wentworth House, belonging to Earl Fitzwilliam; Alton Towers, the country house of the Earl of Shrewsbury; and Chatsworth, the palace of the Duke of Devonshire, where such royal loyal honors were paid to her that she had a foretaste of the "splendor," without the "responsibility," of Queenhood.

The King and Queen gave a brilliant ball in honor of "the thirteenth birthday of their beloved niece, the Princess Victoria," and somewhat later, the little royal lady appeared at a Drawing-room, when she is said to have charmed everybody by her sweet, childish dignity—a sort of quaint queenliness of manner and expression. She was likewise most satisfactory to the most religiously inclined of her subjects who were to be, in her mien and behavior when in the Royal Chapel of St. James, on the interesting occasion of her confirmation. She is said to have gone through the ceremony with "profound thoughtfulness and devout solemnity."

The next glimpse I have of her is at a very different scene—the Ascot races. A brilliant American author, N. P. Willis, who then saw her for the first time, wrote: "In one of the intervals, I walked under the King's stand, and saw Her Majesty the Queen, and the young Princess Victoria, very distinctly. They were leaning over the railing listening to a ballad-singer, and seeming as much interested and amused as any simple country-folk could be. The Queen is undoubtedly the plainest woman in her dominions, but the Princess is much better-looking than any picture of her in the shops, and for the heir to such a crown as that of England, quite unnecessarily, pretty and interesting. She will be sold, poor thing! bartered away by those great-dealers in royal hearts, whose grand calculations will not be much consolation to her if she happens to have a taste of her own."

Little did the wise American poet guess that, away in a little fairy principality of Deutschland, there was a beautiful young fairy prince, being reared by benevolent fairy godmother-grandmothers, especially to disprove all such doleful prophecies, and reverse the usual fate of pretty young Princesses in the case of the "little English mayflower."

Greville relates a little incident which shows that the Princess, when between sixteen and seventeen, and almost in sight of the throne, was still amenable to discipline. He describes a reception of much pomp and ceremony, given to the Duchess and the Princess by the Mayor and other officers of the town of Burghley, followed by a great dinner, which "went off well," except that an awkward waiter, in a spasm of loyal excitement, emptied the contents of a pail of ice in the lap of the Duchess, which, though she took it coolly, "made a great bustle." I am afraid the Princess laughed. Then followed a magnificent ball, which was opened by the Princess, with Lord Exeter for a partner. After that one dance she "went to bed." Doubtless her good mother thought she had had fatigue and excitement enough for one day; but it must have been hard for such a dance-loving girl to take her quivering feet out of the ball-room so early, and for such a grand personage as she already was, just referred to in the Mayor's speech, as "destined to mount the throne of these realms," to be sent away like a child, to mount a solemn, beplumed four- poster, and to try to sleep, with that delicious dance-music still ringing in her ears.

Greville also relates a sad Court story connected with the young Princess, and describes a scene which would be too painful for me to reproduce, except that it reveals, in a striking manner, Victoria's tender love for and close sympathy with her mother. It seems that the King's jealous hostility to the Duchess of Kent had grown with his decay, and strengthened with his senility, till at last it culminated in a sort of declaration of war at his own table. The account is given by Greville *second-hand*, and so, very likely, over-colored, though doubtless true in the main. The King invited the Duchess and Princess to Windsor to join in the celebration of his birthday, which proved to be his last. There was a dinner-party, called "private," but a hundred guests sat down to the table. The Duchess of Kent was given a place of honor on one side of the King, and opposite her sat the Princess Victoria. After dinner Queen Adelaide proposed "His Majesty's health and long life to him," to which that amiable monarch replied by a very remarkable speech. He began by saying that he hoped in God he might live nine months longer, when the Princess would be of age, and he could leave the royal authority in her hands and not in those of a Regent, in the person of a lady sitting near him, etc. Afterwards he said: "I have particularly to complain of the manner in which that young lady (the Princess Victoria) has been kept from my Court. She has been repeatedly kept from my Drawing-rooms, at which she ought always to have been present, but I am resolved that this shall not happen again. I would have *her* know that I am *King*, and am determined to make my authority respected, and for the future I shall insist and command that the Princess do, upon all occasions, appear at my Court, as it is her duty to do."

This pleasant and hospitable harangue, uttered in a loud voice and an excited manner, "produced a decided sensation." The whole company "were aghast." Queen Adelaide, who was amiable and well-bred, "looked in deep distress"; the young Princess burst into tears at the insult offered to her mother; but that mother sat calm and silent, very pale, but proud and erect—Duchess of Duchesses!

CHAPTER VII.

Victoria's first meeting with Prince Albert—She comes of Age—Ball in honor thereof—Illness of King William—His Death—His Habits and Character—The Archbishop of Canterbury and the Lord Chancellor inform Victoria that she is Queen—Her beautiful bearing under the ordeal.

In May, 1836, the Princess saw, for the first time, her cousins, Ernest and Albert, of Saxe-Coburg. These brothers, one eighteen and the other seventeen, are described as charming young fellows, well-bred and carefully educated, with high aims, good, true hearts, and frank, natural manners.

In personal appearance they were very prepossessing. Ernest was handsome, and Albert more than handsome. They were much beloved by their Uncle Leopold, then King of Belgium, and soon endeared themselves to their Aunt Kent and their Cousin Victoria. They spent three weeks at Kensington in daily intercourse with their relatives, and with their father, the Duke of Coburg, were much *fêted* by the royal family. They keenly enjoyed English society and sights, and learned something of English life and character, which to one of them, at least, proved afterwards useful. Indeed this admirable young Prince, Albert, seemed always learning and assimilating new facts and ideas. He had a soul athirst for knowledge.

On May 24, 1837, the Princess Victoria came of age. She was awakened early by a matutinal serenade—a band of musicians piping and harping merrily under her bedroom windows. She received many presents and congratulatory visits, and had the pleasure of knowing that the day was observed as a grand holiday in London and throughout England. Boys were let out of school, and M.P.'s out of Parliament. At night the metropolis was "brilliantly illuminated"—at least so thought those poor, benighted, ante-

17

electrical-light Londoners—and a grand state ball was given in St. James' Palace. Here, for the first time, the Princess took precedence of her mother, and we may believe she felt shy and awkward at such a reversal of the laws of nature and the habits of years. But doubtless the stately Duchess fell back without a sigh, except it were one of joy and gratitude that she had brought her darling on so far safely.

This could hardly have been a very gay state ball, for their Majesties were both absent. The King had that very day been attacked with hayfever, and the Queen had dutifully stayed at home to nurse him. He rallied from this attack somewhat, but never was well again, and in the small hours of June 2d the sailor King died at Royal Windsor, royally enough, I believe, though he had never been a very royal figure or spirit. Of course after he was gone from his earthly kingdom, the most glowing eulogies were pronounced upon him in Parliament, in the newspapers, and in hundreds of pulpits. Even a year later, the Bishop of London, in his sermon at the Queen's coronation, lauded the late King for his "unfeigned religion," and exhorted his "youthful successor" to "follow in his footsteps." Ah, if she had done so, I should not now be writing Her Majesty's Life!

It must be that in a King a little religion goes a long way. The good Bishop and other loyal prelates must have known all about the Fitz- Clarences—those wild "olive branches about the table" of His Majesty; and they were doubtless aware of that little unfortunate habit of profanity, acquired on the high-seas, and scarcely becoming to the Head of the Church; but they, perhaps, considered that His Majesty swore as the sailor, not as the sovereign. He certainly made a good end, hearing many prayers, and joining in them as long as he was able, and devoutly receiving the communion; and what is better, manifesting some tender anxiety lest his faithful wife and patient nurse should do too much and grieve too much for him. When he saw her like to break down, he would say: "Bear up; bear up, Adelaide!" just like any other good husband. William was not a bad King, as Kings went in those days; he was, doubtless, an orthodox churchman, and we may believe he was a good Christian, from his charge to the new Bishop of Ely when he came to "kiss hands" on his preferment: "My lord, I do not wish to interfere in any way with your vote in Parliament, except on one subject—the Jews. I trust I may depend on your always voting against them!"

When the solemn word went through the old Castle of Windsor, "The King is dead!" his most loyal ministers, civil and religious, added under their breath: "Long live the Queen!" and almost immediately the Archbishop of Canterbury and the Lord Chamberlain left Windsor and travelled as fast as post-horses could carry them, to Kensington Palace, which they reached in the gray of the early dawn. Everybody was asleep, and they knocked and rang a long time before they could rouse the porter at the gate, who at last grumblingly admitted them. Then they had another siege in the court-yard; but at length the palace door yielded, and they were let into one of the lower rooms, "where," says Miss Wynn's account, "they seemed forgotten by everybody." They rang the bell, called a sleepy servant, and requested that the special attendant of the Princess Victoria should inform her Royal Highness that they desired an audience on "very important business." More delay, more ringing, more inquiries and directions. At last the attendant of the Princess came, and coolly stated that her Royal Mistress was "in such a sweet sleep she could not venture to disturb her." Then solemnly spoke up the Archbishop: "We are come on business of State, to *the Queen*, and even her sleep must give way." Lo it was out! The startled maid flew on her errand, and so effectually performed it, that Victoria, not daring to keep her visitors waiting longer, hurried into the room with only a shawl thrown over her night- gown, and her feet in slippers. She had flung off her night-cap (young ladies wore night-caps in those queer old times), and her long, light- brown hair was tumbling over her shoulders. So she came to receive the first homage of the Church and the State, and to be hailed "Queen!" and she was Queen of

Great Britain and Ireland, of India and the mighty Colonies! It seems to me that the young girl must have believed herself at that moment only half awake, and still dreaming. The grand, new title, "Your Majesty," must have had a new sound, as addressed to her,—something strange and startling, though very likely she may have often said it over to herself, silently, to get used to it. The first kiss of absolute fealty on her little hand must have thrilled through her whole frame. Some accounts say that as full realization was forced upon her, she burst into tears; others dwell on her marvellous calm and self-possession. I prefer to believe in the tears, not only because the assumption of the "dangerous grandeur of sovereignty" was a solemn and tremendous matter for one so young, but because something of awe and sorrow on hearing of the eternal abdication of that sovereignty, by her rough but not to her unloving old uncle, was natural and womanly, and fitting. I believe that it has not been questioned that the first words of the QUEEN were addressed to the Primate, and that they were simply, "I beg your Grace to pray for me," which the Archbishop did, then and there. Doubtless, also, as related, the first act of her queenly life was the writing of a letter of condolence to Queen Adelaide, in which, after expressing her tender sympathy, she begged her "dear aunt" to remain at Windsor just as long as she might feel inclined. This letter she addressed to "Her Majesty, the Queen." Some one at hand reminded her that the King's widow was now only Queen Dowager. "I am quite aware of that," replied Victoria, "but I will not be the first person to remind her of it." I cannot say how much I like that. Wonderful is the story told by many witnesses of the calmness and gentle dignity of Her Majesty, when a few hours later she met the high officers of the Church and State, Princes and Peers, received their oaths of allegiance and read her first speech from an improvised throne. The Royal Princes, the Dukes of Cumberland and Sussex, Her Majesty's uncles, were the first to be sworn, and Greville says: "As they knelt before her, swearing allegiance and kissing her hand, I saw her blush up to the eyes, as if she felt the contrast between their civil and their natural relations; and this was the only sign of emotion which she evinced."

When she first entered the room she had kissed these old uncles affectionately, walking toward the Duke of Sussex, who was very feeble.

Greville says that she seemed rather bewildered at the multitude of men who came to kiss her hand and kneel to her, among them the conqueror of Napoleon—soldier of soldiers—*the* Duke!—but that she did not make any difference in her manner, or show any especial respect, or condescension in her countenance to any individual, not even to the Premier, Lord Melbourne, for whom she was known to have a great liking, and who was long her trusted friend and favorite Minister.

The Queen was also called upon to take an oath, which was for "the security of the Church of Scotland." This she has most faithfully kept; indeed, she has now and then been reproached by jealous champions of the English Establishment for undue graciousness towards the Kirk and its ministers.

For this grand but solemn ceremony at Kensington—rendered the more solemn by the fact that while it was going on the great bell of St. Paul's was tolling for the dead King,—the young Queen was dressed very simply, in mourning.

She seems to have thought of everything, for she sent for Lord Albemarle, and after reminding him that according to law and precedent she must be proclaimed the next morning at 10 o'clock, from a certain window of St. James' Palace, requested him to provide for her a suitable conveyance and escort. She then bowed gravely and graciously to the Princes, Archbishops and Cabinet Ministers, and left the room, as she had entered it—alone.

19

CHAPTER VIII.

The last day of Victoria's real girlhood—Proclaimed Queen from St. James' Palace—She holds her first Privy Council—Comments upon her deportment by eye-witnesses—Fruits of her mother's care and training.

It seems to me that the momentous day just described was the last of Victoria's real girlhood; that premature womanhood was thrust upon her with all the power, grandeur, and state of a Queen Regnant. I wonder if, weary and nervously exhausted as she must have been, she slept much, when at last she went to bed, probably no longer in her mother's room. I wonder if she did not think, with a sort of fearsome thrill that when the summer sun faded from her sight, it was only to travel all night, lighting her vast dominions and her uncounted millions of subjects; and that, like the splendor of that sun, had become her life—hers, the little maiden's, but just emerging from the shadow of seclusion, and from her mother's protecting care and wise authority, and stepping out into the world by herself!

The next day she went in state to St. James Palace, accompanied by great lords and ladies, and escorted by squadrons of the Life Guards and Blues, and was formally proclaimed from the window of the Presence Chamber, looking out on the court-yard. A Court chronicle states that Her Majesty wore a black silk dress and a little black chip bonnet, and that she looked paler than usual. Miss Martineau, speaking of the scene, says: "There stood the young creature, in simplest mourning, her sleek bands of brown hair as plain as her dress. The tears ran down her cheeks, as Lord Melbourne, standing by her side, presented her to the people as their Sovereign. ... In the upper part of the face she is really pretty, and with an ingenuous, sincere air which seems full of promise."

After the ceremony of proclamation was over, the "little Queen" remained for a few moments at the window, bowing and smiling through her tears at that friendly and enthusiastic crowd of her subjects, and listening to the National Anthem played for the first time for her, then retired, with her mother, who had not been "prominent" during the scene, but who had been observed "to watch her daughter with great anxiety."

At noon the Queen held a Privy Council, at which it was said, "She presided with as much ease as though she had been doing nothing else all her life." At 1 P.M. she returned to Kensington Palace, there to remain in retirement till after the funeral of King William.

It is certain that the behavior of this girl-queen on these first two days of her reign "confounded the doctors" of the Church and State. Greville, who never praises except when praise is wrung out of him, can hardly say enough of her grace and graciousness, calmness and self- possession. He says, also, that her "agreeable expression, with her youth, inspire an excessive interest in all who approach her, and which," he is condescending enough to add, "I can't help feeling myself." He quotes Peel as saying he was "amazed at her manner and behavior; at her apparent deep sense of her situation, her modesty, and at the same time her firmness. She appeared to be awed, but not daunted."

The Duke of Wellington paid a similar tribute to her courage.

Now, if these great men did not greatly idealize her, under the double glamour of gallantry and loyalty, Victoria was a most extraordinary young woman. A few days before the death of the King, Greville wrote: "What renders speculation so easy and events so uncertain is the absolute ignorance of everybody of the character, disposition, and capacity of the Princess. She has been kept in such jealous seclusion by her mother (never having slept out of her bedroom, nor been alone with anybody but herself and, the Baroness Lehzen), that not one of her acquaintance, none of the attendants at Kensington, not even the Duchess of Northumberland, her governess, can have any idea what she is, or what she promises to be." The first day of Victoria's accession he writes: "She appears to act with every sort of good taste and good feeling, as well as good sense, and nothing can be more favorable than the impression she has made, and nothing can promise better than her manner and conduct do... William IV. coming to the throne at the mature age of sixty-five, was so excited by the exaltation that he nearly went mad... The young Queen, who might well be either dazzled or confounded with the grandeur and novelty of her situation, seems neither the one nor the other, and behaves with a propriety and decorum beyond her years."

Doubtless nature was kind to Victoria in the elements of character, but she must have owed very much of this courage, calmness, modesty, simplicity, candor, and sterling good sense to the peculiar, systematic training, the precept and example of her mother, the much-criticised Duchess of Kent, so unpopular at the Court of the late King, and whom Mr. Greville had by no means delighted to honor. Ah, the good, brave Duchess had her reward for all her years of patient exile, all her loving labor and watchful care, and rich compensation for all criticisms, misrepresentations, and fault-finding, that June afternoon, the day of the Proclamation, when she rode from the Palace of St. James to Kensington with her daughter, who had behaved so well—her daughter and her *Queen!*

PART II.

WOMANHOOD AND QUEENHOOD.

CHAPTER IX.

The sovereignty of England and Hanover severed forever—Funeral of King William IV. at Windsor—The Queen and her household remove to Buckingham Palace—She dissolves Parliament—Glowing account of the scene by a contemporary Journal—Charles Sumner a spectator—His eulogy of the Queen's reading.

Ever since the accession to the throne of Great Britain of the House of Brunswick, the Kings of England had also been Kings of Hanover. To carry on the two branches of the royal business simultaneously must have been a little difficult, at least perplexing. It was like riding a "two-horse act," with a wide space between the horses, and a wide difference in their size. But the Salic law prevailed in that little kingdom over there; so its Crown now gently devolved on the head of the male heir- apparent, the Duke of Cumberland, and the quaint old principality parted company with England forever. That is what Her Majesty, Victoria, got, or rather lost, by being a woman. A day or two after her accession, King Ernest called at Kensington Palace to take leave of the Queen, and she dutifully kissed her uncle and brother-sovereign, and wished him God- speed and the Hanoverians joy.

There is no King and no kingdom of Hanover now. When Kaiser William was consolidating so many German principalities into his grand empire, gaily singing the refrain of the song of the old sexton, "*I gather them in! I gather them in!*" he took Hanover, and it has remained under the wing of the great Prussian eagle ever since. It is said that the last King made a gallant resistance, riding into battle at the head of his troops, although he was blind—too blind, perhaps, to see his own weakness. When his throne was taken out from under him, he still clung to the royal title, but his son is known only as the Duke of Cumberland. This Prince, like other small German Princes, made a great outcry against the Kaiser's confiscations, but the inexorable old man still went on piecing an imperial table-cover out of pocket-handkerchiefs.

The young Queen's new Household was considered a very magnificent and unexceptionable one—principally for the rank and character and personal attractions of the ladies in attendance, chief among whom, for beauty and stateliness, was the famous Duchess of Sutherland—certainly one of the most superb women in England, or anywhere else, even at an age when most women are "falling off," and when she herself was a grandmother.

The funeral of King William took place at Windsor in due time, and with all due pomp and ceremony. After lying in state in the splendid Waterloo chamber, under a gorgeous purple pall, several crowns, and other royal insignia, he was borne to St. George's Chapel, followed by Prelates, Peers, and all the Ministers of State, and a solemn funeral service was performed. But what spoke better for him than all these things was the quiet weeping of a good woman up in the Royal Closet, half hidden by the sombre curtains, who looked and listened to the last, and saw her husband let down into the Royal Vault, where, in the darkness, his—their baby- girl awaited him, that Princess with the short life and the long name— poor little Elizabeth Georgina Adelando, whom the childless Queen once hoped to hear hailed "Elizabeth Second of England."

In midsummer the Queen, the Duchess of Kent, and their grand Household moved from Kensington to Buckingham Palace, then new, and an elegant and luxurious royal residence internally, but externally neither beautiful nor imposing. But with the exception of Windsor Castle, none of the English Royal Palaces can be pointed to as models of architectural beauty, or even sumptuous appointments. The palaces of some of our Railway Kings more than rival them in some respects, while those of many of the English nobility are richer in art-treasures and grander in appearance. Kensington Palace was not beautiful, but it was picturesque and historic, which was more than could be said of any of the Georgian structures; there was about it an odor of old royalty, of poetry and romance. The literature and the beauty of Queen Anne's reign were especially associated with it. Queen Victoria was, when she left it, at an age when memories count for little, and doubtless the flitting "*out of the old house into the new*" was effected merrily enough; but long afterwards her orphaned and widowed heart must often have gone back tenderly and yearningly to the scene of many tranquilly happy years with her mother, and of that first little season of companionship with her cousin Albert.

Hardly had she got unpacked and settled in her new home when she had to go through a great parade and ceremony. She went in state to dissolve Parliament. The weather was fine and the whole route from Buckingham Palace to the Parliament House was lined with people, shouting and cheering as the magnificent procession and that brilliant young figure passed slowly along. A London journal of the time gave the following glowing account of her as she appeared in the House of Lords: "At 20 minutes to 3 precisely, Her Majesty, preceded by the heralds and attended by the great officers of state, entered the House—all the Peers and Peeresses, who had risen at the flourish of the trumpets, remaining standing. Her Majesty was attired in a splendid white satin robe, with the ribbon of the Garter crossing her shoulder and a magnificent tiara of diamonds on her head, and wore a necklace and a stomacher of large and costly brilliants. Having ascended the throne, the royal mantle of crimson velvet was placed on Her Majesty's shoulders by the Lords in waiting." And this was the same little girl who, six years before, had bought her own straw hat and carried it home in her hand! I wonder if her own mother did not at that moment have difficulty in believing that radiant and royal creature was indeed her little Victoria!

The account continues: "Her Majesty, on taking her seat, appeared to be deeply moved at the novel and important position in which she was placed, the eyes of the assembled nobility, both male and female, being riveted on her person." I would have wagered a good deal that it was the 'female' eyes that she felt most piercingly. Then it goes on: "Her emotion was plainly discernible in the heavings of her bosom, and the brilliancy of her diamond stomacher, which sparkled out like the sun on the swell of the ocean as the billows rise and fall." So disconcerted was she, it seems, by all this silent, intense observation, that she forgot, nicely seated as she was, that all those Peers and Peeresses were standing, till she was reminded of it by Lord Melbourne, who stood close at her side. Then she graciously inclined her head, and said in rather a low tone, 'My Lords, be seated!' and they sat, and eke their wives and daughters.

"She had regained her self-possession when she came to read her speech, and her voice also, for it was heard all over the great chamber." And it is added: "Her demeanor was characterized by much grace and modest self- possession."

Among the spectators of this rare royal pageant was an American, and a stiff republican, a young man from Boston, called Charles Sumner. He was a scholar, and scholar-like, undazzled by diamonds, admired most Her Majesty's reading. In a letter to a friend he wrote: "I was astonished and delighted. Her voice is sweet and finely modulated, and she pronounced every word distinctly, and with a just regard to its meaning. I think I never heard anything better read in my life than her speech, and I could but respond to Lord Fitz-William's remark to me when the ceremony was over, 'How beautifully she performs!'" How strange it now seems to think of that slight girl of eighteen coming in upon that great assembly of legislators, many of them gray and bald, and pompous and portly, and gravely telling them that they might go home!

CHAPTER X.

Comments upon the young Queen by a contemporaneous writer in *Blackwood*—A new Throne erected for her in Buckingham Palace—A touching Anecdote related by the Duke of Wellington—The Queen insists on paying her Father's Debts—The romantic and passionate interest she evoked—Her mad lover—Attempts upon her life—She takes possession of Windsor Castle.

A writer in *Blackwood*, speaking of the Queen about this time, said: "She is 'winning golden opinions from all sorts of people' by her affability, the grace of her manners, and her prettiness. She is excessively like the Brunswicks and not like the Coburgs. So much the more in her favor. The memory of George III. is not yet passed away, and the people are glad to see his calm, honest, and English physiognomy renewed in his granddaughter."

Her Majesty's likeness to the obstinate but conscientious old king, whose honest face is fast fading quite away from old English half-crowns and golden guineas, has grown with her years.

The same writer, speaking of her personal appearance, says: "She is low of stature, but well formed; her hair the darkest shade of flaxen, and her eyes large and light-blue." A friend who saw her frequently at the time of her accession, said to me the other day: "It is a great mistake to suppose that the Queen owed all the charming portraits which were drawn of her at this time, to the fortunate accident of her birth and destiny. She was really a very lovely girl, with a fine, delicate, rose- bloom complexion, large blue eyes, a fair, broad brow, and an expression of peculiar candor and innocence."

A few days later there was a sensation in Buckingham Palace, at the setting up in the Throne-room of a very magnificent new piece of furniture—a throne of the latest English fashion, but gorgeous enough to have served for the Queen of Sheba, Zenobia, Cleopatra, or Semiramis. It was all crimson velvet and silk, with any amount of gold embroideries, gold lace, gold fringe, ropes, and tassels. The gay young Queen tried it, and said it would do; that she had never sat on a more comfortable throne in all her life.

Two stories of the young Queen have touched me especially—one was related by the Duke of Wellington. A court-martial death sentence was presented by him to her, to be signed. She shrank from the dreadful task, and with tears in her eyes, asked: "Have you nothing to say in behalf of this man?"

"Nothing; he has deserted three times," replied the Iron Duke.

"O, your Grace, think again!"

23

"Well, your Majesty, he certainly is a bad soldier, but there was somebody who spoke as to his good character. He may be a good fellow in civil life."

"O, thank you!" exclaimed the Queen, as she dashed off the word, "Pardoned," on the awful parchment, and wrote beneath it her beautiful signature.

This was not her last act of the kind, and at length Parliament so arranged matters that this fatal signing business could be done by royal commission, ostensibly to "relieve Her Majesty of a painful duty," but really because they could not trust her soft heart. She might have sudden caprices of commiseration which would interfere with stern military discipline, and the honest trade of Mr. Marwood.

The other incident was told by Lord Melbourne. Soon after her accession, in all the dizzy whirl of the new life of splendor and excitement, the young Queen, in an interview with her Prime Minister, said: "I want to pay all that remain of my father's debts. I *must* do it. I consider it a sacred duty." This was, of course, done—the Queen also sending valuable pieces of plate to the largest creditors, as a token of her gratitude. Lord Melbourne said that the childlike directness and earnestness of that good daughter's manner when she thus expressed her royal will and pleasure, brought the tears to his eyes. It seems to me it was almost mission enough for any young woman, to move the hearts of hard old soldiers like Wellington, and *blasé* statesmen like Melbourne— mighty dealers in death and diplomacy, and to bring something like a second youth of romance and chivalrous feeling into worn and worldly hearts everywhere.

I suppose it is impossible for young people of this day, especially Americans, to realize the intense, enthusiastic interest felt forty-six years ago by all classes, and in nearly all countries, in the young English Queen. The old wondered and shook their heads over the mighty responsibility imposed upon her—the young dreamed of her. She almost made real to young girls the wildest romances of fairy lore. She called out such chivalrous feelings in young men that they longed to champion her on some field of battle, or in some perilous knightly adventure. She stirred the hearts and inspired the imaginations of orators and poets.— The great O'Connell, when there was some wild talk of deposing "the all but infant Queen," and putting the Duke of Cumberland in her place, said in his trumpet-like tones, which gave dignity to brogue: "If necessary, I can get 500,000 brave Irishmen to defend the life, the honor, and the person of the beloved young lady by whom England's throne is now filled." Ah, the difference between then and now. "Brave Irishmen" of this day, men who know not O'Connell, are more disposed to blow up the English Queen's palaces, throne and all.

Charles Dickens, who was then full of romance and fancy, was, it is said, possessed by such unresting, wondering thoughts of the fair maiden sovereign, and her magnificent destiny, that for a time his more prosaic friends regarded his enthusiasm as a sort of monomania. Other imaginative young men with heads less "level" (to use an American expression) than that of the great novelist, actually went mad—"clean daft"—the noble passion of loving loyalty ending in an infatuation as absurd as it was unhappy. Before the Queen left Kensington Palace she was much annoyed by the persistent attentions of a provincial admirer, a respectable gentleman, who labored under the hallucination that it was his destiny and his duty to espouse the Queen. He may have felt a preference for private life and rural pleasures, but as a loyal patriot he was ready to make the sacrifice. He drove in a stylish phaeton every morning to the Palace to inquire after Her Majesty's health; and on several days he bribed the men who had charge of the gardens to allow him to assist them in weeding about the piece of water opposite her apartments, in the fond hope of seeing her at the windows, and of her seeing him. Every evening, however, he put on the gentleman of fortune and phaetons, and followed the Queen and the Duchess in their airings. Drove they fast or drove they slow, he was just behind them. On their last drive before removing from Kensington, they alighted in the Harrow Road for a

24

little walk, and were dismayed at seeing this Mr. —— spring from his phaeton, and come eagerly forward. The Duchess sent a page to meet him and beg of him not to annoy Her Majesty by accosting her; but the page was "no let" to him— a whole volume of remonstrance would not have availed. He pressed on, and the august ladies were obliged to re-enter their carriage, and return to Kensington. When on the next morning they removed from the old home, Mr. —— was at the gate in his phaeton, and drove before them to Buckingham Palace, and was there to give them a gracious welcome. He haunted Pimlico for a time, but his friends finally got possession of him and suppressed him, and so ended his "love's young dream."

It is likely that the merry young Queen laughed at the absurd demonstrations and amatory effusions of her demented admirers; but when, after her marriage, and her appearing always in public with the handsomest Prince in Christendom at her side, such monomaniacs grew desperate and took to shooting, the matter became serious. Then no more gentlemen in phaetons menaced her peace; her demented followers were poor wretches—so poor that sometimes, after investing in pistols, they had not a six-pence left for ammunition. One, a distraught Fenian, pointed at her a broken, harmless weapon, charged with a scrap of red rag. Another, a humpbacked lad, named Bean, loaded his with paper and a few bits of an old clay pipe. Bean escaped for a time, and it is said that for several days there were "hard lines" for all the poor humpbacks of London. Scores of them were arrested. No unfortunate thus deformed, could appear in the streets without danger of a policeman smiting him on the shoulders, right in the tender spot, with a rough, "You are my prisoner." Life became a double burden to the poor fellows till Bean was caught. But to return to the young Queen, in her happy, untroubled days.

In August she took possession of Windsor Castle, amid great rejoicing. The Duchess, her mother, came also; this time not to be reproached or insulted. They soon had company—a lot of Kings and Queens, among them "Uncle Leopold" and his second wife, a daughter of Louis Philippe of France.

The royal young house-keeper seems keenly to have enjoyed showing to her visitors her new home, her little country place up the Thames. She conducted them everywhere,

"Up-stairs, down-stairs, and in my lady's chamber,"

peeping into china and silver closets, spicy store-rooms, and huge linen chests smelling of lavender.

Soon after came a triumphal progress to Brighton, during which the royal carriage passed under an endless succession of triumphal arches, and between ranks on ranks of schoolchildren, strewing roses and singing pæans. At Brighton there was an immense sacrifice of the then fashionable and costly flower, the dahlia, no fewer than twenty thousand being used for decorative purposes. But a sadder because a vain sacrifice on this occasion, was of flowers of rhetoric. An address, the result of much classical research and throes of poetic labor, and marked by the most effusive loyalty, was to have been presented to Her Majesty at the gates of the Pavilion, but by some mistake she passed in without waiting for it.

About this time the Lunatic Asylums began to fill up. Within one week two mad men were arrested, proved insane, and shut up for threatening the life of the Queen and the Duchess of Kent. So Victoria's life was not all arched over with dahlia-garlands, and strewn with roses, nor were her subjects all Sunday-school scholars.

CHAPTER XI.

Banquet in Guildhall—Victoria's first Christmas at Windsor Castle as Queen—Mrs. Newton Crosland's reminiscences—Coolness of Actors and

Quakers amid the general enthusiasm—Issue of the first gold Sovereigns bearing Victoria's head.

On Lord Mayor's Day, the Queen went in state to dine with her brother- monarch, the King of "Great London Town." It was a memorable, magnificent occasion. The Queen was attended by all the great ladies and gentlemen of her Court, and followed by an immense train of members of the royal family, ambassadors, cabinet ministers and nobility generally—in all, two hundred carriages of them. The day was a general holiday, and the streets all along the line of the splendid procession were lined with people half wild with loyal excitement, shouting and waving hats and handkerchiefs. It may have been on this day that Lord Albemarle got off his famous pun. On the Queen saying to him, "I wonder if my good people of London are as glad to see me as I am to see them?" he replied by pointing to the letters "V. R." "Your Majesty can see their loyal cockney answer-'*Ve are.*'"

One account states that, "the young sovereign was quite overcome by the enthusiastic outbursts of loyalty which greeted her all along the route," but a description of the scene sent me by a friend, Mrs. Newton Crosland, the charming English novelist and poet, paints her as perfectly composed. My friend says: "I well remember seeing the young Queen on her way to dine with the Lord Mayor, on the 9th of November, 1837, the year of her accession. The crowd was so great that there were constant stoppages, and, luckily for me, one of them occurred just under the window of a house in the Strand, where I was a spectator. I shall never forget the appearance of the maiden-sovereign. Youthful as she was, she looked every inch a Queen. Seated with their backs to the horses were a lady and gentleman, in full Court-dress—(the Duchess of Sutherland, Mistress of the Robes—and the Earl of Albemarle, Master of the Horse), and in the centre of the opposite seat, a little raised, was the Queen. All I saw of her dress was a mass of pink satin and swan's-down. I think she wore a large cape or wrap of these materials. The swan's-down encircled her throat, from which rose the fair young face—the blue eyes beaming with goodness and intelligence—the rose-bloom of girlhood on her cheeks, and her soft, light brown hair, on which gleamed a circlet of diamonds, braided as it is seen in the early portraits. Her small, white-gloved hands were reposing easily in her lap.

"On this occasion not only were the streets thronged, but every window in the long line of the procession was literally filled, while men and boys were seen in perilous positions on roofs and lamp-posts, trees and railings. Loud and hearty cheers, so unanimous they were like one immense multitudinous shout, heralded the royal carriage.

"A little before this date, a story was told of the lamentations of the Queen's coachman. He declared that he had driven Her Majesty for six weeks, without once being able to see her. Of course he could not turn his head or his eyes from his horses."

At Temple Bar—poor, old Temple Bar, now a thing of the past!—the Queen was met by the Lord Mayor, who handed her the city keys and sword, which she returned to his keeping—a little further on, the scholars of Christ's Hospital—the "Blue-Coat Boys," offered her an address of congratulation, saying how glad they were to have a woman to rule over them, which was a good deal for boys to say, and also sung the National Anthem with a will.

The drawing-room of Guildhall was fitted up most gorgeously. Here the address of the city magnates was read and replied to,—and here in the midst of Princes and nobles, Her Majesty performed a brave and memorable act. She knighted Sheriff Montefiore, the first man of his race to receive such an honor from a British sovereign, and Sir Moses Montefiore, now nearly a centenarian, has ever since, by a noble life and good works, reflected only honor on his Queen. But ah, what would her uncle, the late King, have said, had he seen her profaning a Christian sword by laying it on the shoulders of a Jew! He would rather have used it on the unbeliever's ears, after Peter's fashion.

After this ceremony, they all passed into the Great Hall, which had been marvellously metamorphosed, by hangings and gildings, and all sorts of magnificent decorations, by mirrors and lusters, and the display of vast quantities of gold and silver plate—much of it lent for the occasion by noblemen and private gentlemen, but rivalled in splendor and value by the plate of the Corporation and the City Companies. From the roof hung two immense chandeliers of stained glass and prisms, which with the flashing of innumerable gas-jets, lighting up gorgeous Court-dresses, and the most superb old diamonds of the realm, made up a scene of dazzling splendor, of enchantment, which people who were there go wild over to this day. Poets say it was like a vision of fairyland, among the highest circles of that most poetic kingdom—and they know. I think a poet must have managed the musical portion of the entertainment, for when Victoria appeared sweet voices sang—

"At Oriana's presence all things smile!"

and presently—

"Oh happy fair!
Your eyes are lode-stars and your tongue's sweet air,
More tunable than lark to shepherd's ear,
When wheat is green, when hawthorn buds appear."

There was a raised platform at the east end of the hall, and on it the throne, a beautiful state-chair, of dainty proportions, made expressly for that fairy Princess, who took her seat thereon amid the most joyous acclamations. On the platform before her, was placed the royal table, decorated with exquisite flowers, and covered with a costly, gold-fringed damask cloth, on which were served the most delicate viands and delicious fruits, in season and out of season. Ah, as the young Queen, seated up there, received the homage of the richly-robed Aldermen, and the resplendent Sheriffs, and that effulgent Lord Mayor, she must have fancied herself something more than a fairy Princess,—say, an Oriental goddess being adored and sacrificed to by gorgeous Oriental Princes, Sultans and Satraps, Pashas, Padishas, and the Grand-Panjandrum himself.

After the dinner, an imposing personage, called the Common Crier, strode into the middle of the hall, and solemnly cried out: "The Right Honorable the Lord Mayor gives the health of our Most Gracious Sovereign, Queen Victoria!" This, of course, was drunk with all the honors, and extra shouts that made the old hall ring. The Queen rose and bowed her thanks, and then the Common Crier announced—Her Majesty's toast: "The Lord Mayor, and prosperity to the City of London." The Queen, it is stated, honored this toast in sherry one hundred and twenty years old—liquid gold! Very gracious of her if she furnished the sherry. I hope, at all events, she drank it with reverence. Why, when that old wine was bottled, Her Majesty's grandfather lacked some twenty years of being born, and the American Colonies were as loyal as London;—then the trunk of the royal old Bourbon tree, whose last branch death lopped away but yesterday at Frohsdorf, seemed solid enough, though rotten at the core; and, the great French Revolution was undreamed of, except in the seething brain of some wild political theorist, or in some poor peasant's nightmare of starvation. When that old wine was bottled, Temple Bar, under the garlanded arch of which Her Majesty had just passed so smilingly, was often adorned with gory heads of traitors, and long after that old wine was bottled, men and women could be seen of a Friday, dangling from the front of Newgate prison, and swinging in the morning air, like so many ghastly pendulums.

This year 1837, Victoria spent her first Christmas as a Queen at Windsor, right royally I doubt not, and I think it probable she received a few presents. A few days before, she had gone in state to Parliament, to give her assent to the New Civil List Act-not a hard duty for her to perform, it would seem, as that act settled on her for life an annual income of £385,000. Let Americans who begrudge our President his $50,000, and wail over our

27

taxation, just put that sum into dollars. The English people did not grumble at this grant, as they had grumbled over the large sums demanded by Her Majesty's immediate predecessors. They knew it would not be recklessly and wickedly squandered, and they liked to have their bonnie young Queen make a handsome appearance among crowned heads. She had not then revealed those strong and admirable traits of character which later won their respect and affection,—but they were fond of her, and took a sort of amused delight in her, as though they, were all children, and she a wonderful new doll, with new-fashioned talking and walking arrangements. The friend from whom I have quoted—Mrs. Crosland— writes me: "I consider that it would be impossible to exaggerate the enthusiasm of the English people on the accession of Queen Victoria to the throne. To be able at all to understand it, we must recollect the sovereigns she succeeded—the Sailor-King, a most commonplace old man, with 'a head like a pine-apple'; George IV., a most unkingly king, extremely unpopular, except with a small party, of High Tories; and poor George III., who by the generation Victoria followed, could only be remembered as a frail, afflicted, blind old man—for a long period shut up at Kew, and never seen by his people. It was not only that Victoria was a really lovely girl, but that she had the *prestige* of having been brought up as a Liberal, and then she kept the hated Duke of Cumberland from the throne. Possibly he was not guilty of half the atrocious sins attributed to him, but I do not remember any royal personage so universally hated."

It was fear of this bogie of a Cumberland that made the English people anxious for the early marriage of the Queen, and yet caused them to dread it, for the fate of poor Princess Charlotte had not been forgotten. But I do not think that political or dynastic questions had much to do with the popularity of the young Queen. It was the resurrection of the dead dignity of the Royal House of Brunswick, in her fair person—the resuscitation of the half-dead principle of loyalty in the hearts of her people. Of her Majesty's subjects of the better class, actors and quakers alone seem to have taken her accession with all its splendid accessions, coolly,—the former, perhaps, because much mock royalty had somehow cheapened the real thing, and the latter because trained from infancy to disregard the pomps and show of this world. Macready jots down among the little matters in his "Diary," the fact of Her Majesty coming to his theatre, and waiting awhile after the play to see him and congratulate him. He speaks of her as "a pretty little girl," and does not seem particularly "set up" by her compliments. Joseph Sturge, the eminent and most lovable philanthropist of Birmingham,—a "Friend indeed" to all "in need,"—waited on Her Majesty, soon after her accession, as one of a delegation of the Society of Friends. Some years after, he related the circumstance to me, and simply described her to me as "a nice, pleasant, modest young woman,—graceful, though a little shy, and on the whole, comely."

"Did you kiss her hand?" I asked. "O yes, and found that act of homage no hardship, I assure thee. It was a fair, soft, delicate little hand."

I afterwards regretted that I had not asked him what he did with his broad-brimmed hat when he was about to be presented, knowing that the principles of Fox and Penn forbade his removing that article in homage to any human creature; but I have just discovered in a volume of Court Records, that "the deputation from the Society of Friends, commonly called Quakers, were uncovered, according to custom, by the Yeoman of the Guard." As they were all non-resistants, they doubtless bore the indignity passively and placidly. Moreover, they all bowed, if they did not kneel, before the throne on which their Queen was seated, and as I said kissed her hand, in token of their friendly fealty.

In June, 1838, were issued the first gold sovereigns, bearing the head of the Queen—the same spirited young head that we see now on all the modern gold and silver pieces of the realm. That on the copper is a little different, but all are pretty—so pretty that Her

Majesty's loyal subjects prefer them to all other likenesses, even poor men feeling that they cannot have too many of them.

CHAPTER XII.

The Coronation.

The coronation was fixed for June 28, 1838 a little more than a year from the accession.

The, Queen had been slightly troubled at the thought of some of the antiquated forms of that grand and complicated ceremony—for instance, the homage of the Peers, spiritual and temporal. As the rule stood, they were all required after kneeling to her, and pledging their allegiance, to rise and kiss her on the left cheek. She might be able to bear up under the salutes of those holy old gentlemen, the archbishops and bishops—but the anticipation of the kisses of all the temporal Peers, old and young, was enough to appall her—there were six hundred of them. So she issued a proclamation excusing the noble gentlemen from that onerous duty, and at the coronation only the Royal Dukes, Sussex and Cambridge, kissed the Queen's rosy cheek, by special kinship privilege. The others had to be content with her hand. The other omitted ceremony was one which formerly took place in Westminster Hall—consisting chiefly of the appearance of a knight armed, mailed and mounted, who as Royal Champion proceeded to challenge the enemies of the new Sovereign to mortal combat. This, which had appeared ridiculous in the case of the burly George IV., would have been something pretty and poetic in that of the young maiden-Queen, but she doubtless felt that as every Englishman was disposed to be her champion, the old form would be the idlest, melodramatic bravado.

The crown which had fitted George and William was too big and heavy for their niece—so it was taken to pieces, and the jewels re-set in a way to greatly reduce the size and weight. A description now before me, of the new crown is too dazzling for me to transcribe. I must keep my eyes for plainer work; but I can give the value of the bauble— £112,760!—and this was before the acquisition of the koh-i-noor.

Of the coronation I will try to give a clear, if not a full account.

It was a wonderful time in London when that day of days was ushered in, by the roar of cannon from the grim old Tower, answered by a battery in St. James' Park. Such a world of people everywhere! All Great Britain and much of the Continent seemed to have emptied themselves into this metropolis, which overflowed with a surging, murmuring tide of humanity. Ah me, how much of that eager, noisy life is silent and forgotten now!

There may have before been coronations surpassing that of Victoria in scenic splendor, if not in solid magnificence-that of the first Napoleon and his Empress, perhaps-but there has been nothing so grand as a royal pageant seen since, until the crowning of the present Russian Emperor at Moscow, where the almost intolerable splendor was seen against a dark background of tragic possibilities. This English coronation was less brilliant, perhaps, but also less barbaric than that august, overpowering ceremony over which it seemed there might hover "perturbed spirits" of men slain in mad revolts against tyranny—of youths and women done to death on the red scaffold, in dungeons, in midnight mines, and Siberian snows; and about which there surely lurked the fiends of dynamite. But this pure young girl, trusting implicitly in the loving loyalty of her subjects—relying on Heaven for help and guidance, lifted to the throne by the Constitution and the will of a free people, as conquerors have been upborne on shields, what had she to fear? A very different and un- nihilistic "cloud of witnesses" was hers, we may believe. If ever there was a mortal state-occasion for the immortals to be abroad, it was this.

The great procession started from Buckingham Palace at about 10 o'clock. The first two state carriages, each drawn by six horses, held the Duchess of Kent and her attendants. The Queen's mother, regally attired, was enthusiastically cheered all along the way. The

Queen was, of course, in the grand state coach, which is mostly gilding and glass—a prodigiously imposing affair. It was drawn by eight cream-colored horses—great stately creatures—with white flowing manes, and tails like mountain cascades. Many battalions and military bands were stationed along the line, presenting arms and playing the National Anthem, "And the People, O the People!" Every window, balcony, and door-step was swarming, every foot of standing room occupied—even on roofs and chimneys. Ladies and children waved handkerchiefs and dropped flowers from balconies, and the shouts from below and the shouts from above seemed to meet and break into joyous storm-bursts in the air. Accounts state that Her Majesty "looked exceedingly well, and that she seemed in excellent spirits, and highly delighted with the imposing scene and the enthusiasm of her subjects." One would think she might have been.

She had a great deal to go through with that day. She must have rehearsed well, or she would have been confused by the multiform ceremonials of that grand spectacular performance. The scene, as she entered Westminster Abbey, might well have startled her out of her serene calm, but it didn't. On each side of the nave, reaching from the western door to the organ screen, were the galleries, erected for the spectators. These were all covered with crimson cloth fringed with gold. Underneath them were lines of foot-guards, very martial-looking, fellows. The old stone floor, worn with the tread of Kings' coronations and funeral processions, was covered with matting, and purple and crimson cloth. Immediately under the central tower of the Abbey, inside the choir, five steps from the floor, on a carpet of purple and gold, was a platform covered with cloth of gold, and on it was the golden "Chair of Homage." Within the chancel, near the altar, stood the stiff, quaint old chair in I which all the sovereigns of England since Edward the Confessor have been crowned. Cloth of gold quite concealed the "chunk of old red sandstone," called the "stone of Scone," on which the ancient Scottish Kings were crowned, and which the English seem to keep and use for luck. There were galleries on galleries upholstered in crimson cloth, and splendid tapestries, wherein sat members of Parliament and foreign Princes and Embassadors. In the organ loft were singers in white, and instrumental performers in scarlet —all looking very fine and festive; and up very high was a band of trumpeters, whose music, pealing over the heads of the people, produced, at times, a wonderful effect.

Fashionable people had got up early for once. Many were at the Abbey doors long before 5 o'clock, and when the Queen arrived at 11:30, hundreds of delicate ladies in full evening-dress, had been waiting for her for seven long hours. The foreign Princes and Embassadors were in gorgeous costumes; and there was the Lord Mayor in all his glory, blinding to behold. His most formidable rival was Prince Esterhazy, who sparkled with costly jewels from his head down to his boots-looking as though he had been snowed upon with pearls, and had also been caught out in a rain of diamonds, and had come in dripping. All these grand personages and the Peers and Peeresses were so placed as to have a perfect view of the part of the minster in which the coronation took place-called, in the programme, "the Theatre."

The Queen came in about the middle of the splendid procession. In her royal robe of crimson velvet, furred with ermine, and trimmed with gold lace, wearing the collars of her orders, and on her head a circlet of gold-her immense train borne by eight very noble young ladies, she is said to have looked "truly royal," though so young, and only four feet eight inches in height. As she entered the Abbey, the orchestra and choir broke out into the National Anthem. They performed bravely, but were scarcely heard for the mighty cheers which went up from the great assembly, making the old minster resound in all its aisles and arches and ancient chapels. Then, as she advanced slowly towards the choir, the anthem, "*I was glad*" was sung, and after that, the sweet-voiced choir-boys of Westminster chanted like so many white-gowned, sleek-headed angels, "*Vivat Victoria*

30

Regina!" Ah, then she felt very solemnly that she was Queen; and moving softly to a chair placed between the Chair of Homage and the altar, she knelt down on the "faldstool" before it, and meekly said her prayers.

When the boys had finished their glad anthem, the Archbishop of Canterbury, with several high officers of state, moved to the east side of the theatre, when the Primate, in a loud voice, said: "I here present unto you Queen Victoria, the undoubted Queen of this realm, wherefore all you who are come this day to your homage, are you willing to do the same?"

It seems a little confused, but the people understood it, and shouted, "God save Queen Victoria!" This "recognition," as it was called, was repeated at the south, west, and north sides of the "theatre," and every time was answered by that joyous shout, and by the pealing of trumpets and the beating of drums. The Queen stood throughout this ceremony, each time turning her head towards the point from which the recognition came.

One may almost wonder if all those loyal shouts and triumphant trumpetings and drum-beatings did not trouble somewhat the long quiet of death in the dusky old chapels in which sleep the fair Queen Eleanor, and the gracious Philippa, and valiant Elizabeth, and hapless Mary Stuart.

Then followed a great many curious rites and ceremonies of receiving and presenting offerings; and many prayers and the reading of the Litany, and the preaching of the sermon, in which the poor Queen was exhorted to "follow in the footsteps of her predecessor"—which would have been to walk "sailor-fashion" morally. Then came the administration of the oath. After having been catechised by the Archbishop in regard to the Established Church, Her Majesty was conducted to the altar, where kneeling, and laying her hand on the Gospels in the great Bible, she said, in clear tones, silvery yet solemn: "The things which I have here before promised, I will perform and keep. So help me God!"

She then kissed the book, and after that the hymn, "*Come, Holy Ghost, our souls inspire*" was sung by the choir, the Queen still kneeling.

I read the other day that the Duke of Connaught (Prince Arthur), on visiting Norwich Cathedral, was shown the very Bible on which his mother took her well-kept coronation oath, forty-five years ago. It was a most solemn pledge, and yet it was all comprehended in the little girl Victoria's promise to her governess, "I will be good."

Her Majesty next seated herself in St. Edward's chair; a rich cloth of gold was held over her head, and the Archbishop anointed her with holy oil, in the form of a cross. Then followed more prayers, more forms and ceremonies, the presentation of swords and spurs, and such like little feminine adornments, the investing with the Imperial robe, the sceptre and the ring, the consecration and blessing of the new crown, and at last the crowning. In this august ceremony three Archbishops, two Bishops, a Dean, and several other clergymen were somehow employed. The task was most religiously performed. It was the Primate of all England who reverently placed the crown on that reverent young head. The moment this was done all the Peers and Peeresses, who, with their coronets in their hands, or borne by pages at their sides, had been intently watching the proceedings, crowned themselves, shouting, "God save the Queen!" while again trumpets pealed forth, and drums sounded, and the far-off Tower and Park guns, fired by signal, boomed over the glad Capital.

It is stated that the most magically beautiful effect of all was produced by the Peeresses, in suddenly and simultaneously donning their coronets. It was as though the stars had somehow kept back their radiance till the young moon revealed herself in all her silver splendor.

31

Then came the exhortation, an anthem, and a benediction, and after a few more forms and pomps, the Queen was conducted to the Chair of Homage. Before the next long ceremony began, the Queen handed her two sceptres to two of the lords in attendance, to keep for her, as quietly as any other girl might hand over to a couple of dangling young gentlemen her fan and bouquet to hold for her, while she drew on her gloves.

The Lords Spiritual, headed by the Primate, began the homage by kneeling, and kissing the Queen's hand. Then came the Dukes of Sussex and Cambridge, who, removing their coronets, and touching them to the Crown, solemnly pledged their allegiance, and kissed their niece on the left cheek. Her manner to them was observed to be very affectionate. Then the other Dukes, and Peers on Peers did homage by kneeling, touching coronet to crown, and kissing that little white hand. When the turn of the Duke of Wellington came, the entire assembly broke into applause; and yet he was not the hero of the day, but an older and far more infirm Peer, Lord Rolle, who mounted the steps with difficulty, and stumbling at the top, fell, and rolled all the way back to the floor, where "he lay at the bottom of the steps, coiled up in his robes." At sight of the accident the Queen rose from her throne, and held out her hands as though to help him. It was a pretty incident, not for the poor Peer, but as showing Her Majesty's impulsive kindness of heart. The old nobleman was not hurt, but quickly unwound himself, rose, mounted the steps, and tried again and again to touch the crown with the coronet in his weak, uncertain hand, every plucky effort being hailed with cheers. At length the Queen, smiling, gave him her hand to kiss, dispensing with the form of touching her crown. Miss Martineau, who witnessed the scene, states that a foreigner who was present was made to believe by a wag that this ludicrous tumble was a part of the regular programme, and that the Lords Rolle held their title on condition of performing that feat at every coronation, Rolle meaning roll.

This most tedious ceremony over, finishing up with more anthems, trumpets, drums, and shouts, the Sacrament was administered to the Queen —she discrowning herself, and kneeling while she partook of the holy elements. Then a re-crowning, a re-enthronement, more anthems, and the blessed release of the final benediction. Passing into King Edward's chapel, the Queen changed the Imperial for the Royal robe of purple velvet, and passed out of the Abbey, wearing her crown, bearing the sceptre in her right hand, and the orb in her left, and so got into her carriage, and drove home through the shouting multitude. It is stated that Her Majesty did not seem exhausted, though she was observed to put her hand to her head frequently, as though the crown was not, after all, a very comfortable fit.

After reigning more than a year, she had been obliged to spend nearly five fatiguing hours in being finished as a Queen. How strange it all seems to us American Republicans, who make and unmake our rulers with such expedition and scant ceremony.

CHAPTER XIII.

Pictures and descriptions of the Queen—Her love of pets—Her passion for horseback exercise—Her spirited behavior in the first change of her Ministers.

In the Hall of the St. George's Society of Philadelphia there is a very interesting picture by the late Mr. Sully of Queen Victoria in her coronation robes. It is life-size, and represents her as mounting the steps of the throne, her head slightly turned, and looking back over the left shoulder. It seems to me that Her Majesty should own this picture, for it is an exquisite specimen of Mr. Sully's peculiar coloring, and a very lovely portrait. Here is no rigidity, no constraint, no irksome state. There is a springy, exultant vitality in the bearing of the graceful figure, and the light poise of the head, while in the complexion there is a tender softness and a freshness of tints belonging only to the dewy morning of life. The princeliness of youth, the glow of joy and hope overtop and outshine the crown which she wears as lightly as though it were a May-queen's Coronal of roses; and the dignity of simple girlish purity envelops her more royally than velvet and ermine. The eyes have the softness of morning skies and spring violets, and the smile hovering about the red lips, a little parted, is that of an unworn heart and an eager, confident spirit. This was the first portrait of the young Queen I ever saw, and still seems to me the loveliest.

Another American artist, Mr. Leslie, painted a large picture of the coronation, which Her Majesty purchased. As he was to paint the scene, he was provided with a very good seat near the throne—so near that he said he could plainly see, when she came to sign her coronation oath, that she wrote a large, bold hand, doing credit to her old writing master, Mr. Steward.

In his recollections he says: "I don't know why, but the first sight of her in her robes of state brought tears into my eyes, and it had this effect upon many people; she looked almost like a child." Campbell, the poet, is related to have said to a friend: "I was at Her Majesty's coronation in Westminster Abbey, and she conducted herself so well during the long and fatiguing ceremony that I shed tears many times."

Carlyle said at the time, with a shake of his craggy, shaggy head: "Poor little Queen! she is at an age at which a girl can hardly be trusted to choose a bonnet for herself, yet a task is laid upon her from which an archangel might shrink.":

And yet, according to Earl Russell, this "poor little Queen," over whom the painters and poets wept, and the great critic "roared gently" his lofty commiseration, informed her anxious mother that she "ascended the throne without alarm." Victoria, if reminded of this in later years, might have said, "They who know nothing, fear nothing"; and yet the very vagueness, as well as vastness, of the untried life would have appalled many spirits.

The Queen was certainly a very valiant little woman, but there would have been something unnatural, almost uncanny, about her had the regal calm and religious seriousness which marked her mien during those imposing rites, continued indefinitely, and it is right pleasant to read in the reminiscences of Leslie, how the child in her broke out when all the magnificent but tiresome parade, all the grand stage-business with those heavy actors, was over. The painter says: "She is very fond of dogs, and has one favorite little spaniel, who is always on the lookout for her return when she is from home. She had, of course, been separated from him on that day longer than usual, and when the state-coach drove up to the Palace steps she heard him barking joyously in the hall, and exclaimed, 'There's Dash,' and was in a hurry to doff her crown and royal robe, and lay down the sceptre and the orb, which she carried in her hands, and go and give Dash his bath."

I hope this story is literally true, for I have a strong impression that it was this peculiar love of pets, this sense of companionship with intelligent, affectionate animals, especially dogs and horses, that with an ever-fresh delight in riding and dancing, healthful sports and merry games, was the salvation of the young Queen. Without such vents, the mighty responsibility of her dizzy position, the grandeur, the dignity, the decorum, the awful etiquette would have killed her—or at least, puffed her up with pride, or petrified her with formality. Sir John Campbell wrote of her at this time: "She is as merry and playful as a kitten."—I hope she loved kittens! Again he says: "The Queen was in great spirits, and danced with more than usual gaiety, a romping, country-dance, called the Tempest."

In addition to this girlish gaiety, Victoria seems always to have had a vein of un-Guelph-like humor, a keen sense of the ludicrous, a delicious enjoyment of fun, which are among Heaven's choicest blessings to poor mortals, royal or republican. Prince Albert's sympathy with her love of innocent amusement, and her delight in the absurdities and drolleries of animal as well as of human life and character, was one and perhaps not the weakest of the ties which bound her to him.

With the young Queen equestrian exercise was more than a pastime, it was almost a passion. She rode remarkably well, and in her gratitude for this beautiful accomplishment,—rarer even in England than people think—she wished as soon as she came to the throne, to give her riding-master, Fozard, a suitable position near her person, something higher than that of a groom. She was told that there was no situation vacant that he could fill. "Then I will create one," she said, and dubbed him "Her Majesty's Stirrup holder." I would have done more for him—made him Master of the Horse, in place of Lord Albemarle, who always rolled along in the royal carriage, or created for him the office of Lord High Equerry of the Realm.

N. P. Willis, in his delightful "Pencilings By the Way," gives a bright glimpse of the Queen on horseback. It was in Hyde Park, and he saye the party from the Palace came on so fast that the scarlet-coated outriders had difficulty in clearing the track of the other equestrians. Her Majesty has always liked to go fast by horse or steam-power, as though determined not to let Time get ahead of her, for all his wings.

The poet then adds: "Her Majesty rides quite fearlessly and securely. I met her party full gallop near the centre of Rotten Row. On came the Queen, on a dun-colored, highly-groomed horse, with her Prime Minister on one side of her, and Lord Byron on the other; her *cortège* of Maids of Honor, and Lords and Ladies of the Court checking their spirited horses, and preserving always a slight distance between themselves and Her Majesty. ... Victoria's round, plump figure looks exceedingly well in her dark green riding-dress. ... She rode with her mouth open, and seemed exhilarated with pleasure."

This was in 1839. Some years later, a young American writer, who shall be nameless, but who was as passionate a lover of horses as the Queen herself, wrote a sort of pæan to horseback-riding. She began by telling her friends, all whom it might concern, that when she was observed to be low in her mind—when she seemed "weary of life," and to "shrink from its strife"—when, in short, things didn't go well with her generally, they were not to come to her with the soft tones or the tears of sympathy; then she went on thus, rather pluckily, I think:

"No counsel I ask, and no pity I need,
But bring me, O bring me, my gallant young steed,
With his high-arched neck and his nostril spread wide;
His eye full of fire, and his step full of pride.
As I spring to his back, as I seize the strong rein,
The strength to my spirit returneth again,
The bonds are all broken that fettered my mind,
And my cares borne away on the wings of the wind,—
My pride lifts its head, for a season, bowed down,
And the queen in my nature now puts on her crown."

Now if the simple American girl prepared for a lonely gallop through the woods, could so have thrilled with the fulness, joy, and strength of young life; could have felt so royal, mounted on a half-broken, roughly- groomed western colt (for that's what the "steed" really was), with few fine points and no pedigree to speak of—what must the glorious exercise have been to that great little Queen, re-enthroned on thoroughbred, "highly-groomed," magnificent English horse-flesh?

Her Majesty has always been constant in her equine loves. Six of her saddle-horses, splendidly caparisoned, walked proudly, as so many Archbishops, in the coronation procession; and in the royal stables of London and Windsor, her old favorites have been most tenderly cared for. When she could no longer use them, she still petted them, and never reproached them for having "outlived their usefulness."

34

Another writer from America, James Gordon Bennett, sent home, this coronation year, some very pleasant descriptions of the Queen. At the opera he had his first sight of her. "About ten o'clock, when the opera was half through, the royal party entered. 'There! there! there!' exclaimed a young girl behind me—'there's the Queen!' looking eagerly up to the royal box. I looked too, and saw a fair, light-haired little girl, dressed with great simplicity, in white muslin, with hair plain, a blue ribbon at the back, enter the box and take her seat, half hid in the red drapery at the corner remote from the stage. The Queen is certainly very simple in her appearance; but I am not sure that this very simplicity does not set off to advantage her fair, pretty, pleasant, little round Dutch face. Her bust is extremely well-proportioned, and her complexion very fair. There is a slight parting of the rosy lips, between which you can see little nicks of something like very white teeth. The expression of her face is amiable and good-tempered. I could see nothing like that awful majesty, that mysterious something which doth hedge a Queen. ... During the performance, the Queen would now and then draw aside the curtain and gaze back at the audience, with that earnestness and curiosity which any young girl might show."

Mr. Bennett gave other descriptions of the Queen as he saw her driving in the Park. He wrote: "I had been taking a walk over the interior of the Park, gazing listlessly at the crowd of carriages as they rolled by. Just as I was entering the arched gateway to depart, a sensation spread through the crowd which filled that part of the promenade. 'The Queen! the Queen!' flew from lip to lip. In an instant two outriders shot through the gate; near Apsley House, followed by a barouche and four, carrying the Queen and three of her suite. She sat on the right hand of the back seat, leaning a good deal back. She was, as usual, dressed very simply, in white, with a plain straw, or Leghorn bonnet, and her veil was thrown aside. She carried a green parasol."

Ah, why *green*, O Queen? Later that afternoon he saw her again, going at a slower rate, holding up that green parasol, bowing right and left and smiling, as the crowd saluted and cheered. The Queen does not bow and smile so much nowadays, but then she no longer carries a green parasol.

N. P. Willis also saw the young sovereign at the opera, and dashes off a poet's vivid sketch of her:

"In her box to the left of me sat the Queen, keeping time with her fan to the singing of Pauline Garcia, her favorite Minister, Lord Melbourne, standing behind her chair, and her maids of honor grouped around her— herself the youthful, smiling, admired sovereign of the most powerful nation on earth. The Queen's face has thinned and grown more oval since I saw her four years ago as the Princess Victoria. She has been compelled to think since then, and such exigencies in all stations in life work out the expression of the face. She has now what I should pronounce a decidedly intellectual countenance, a little petulant withal when she turns to speak, but on the whole quite beautiful enough for a virgin Queen. She was dressed less gaily than many others around her."

I have given much space to these personal descriptions of Queen Victoria as she appeared in those first two years of her Queenhood, because they are still to the world— the world of young people, at least—the most interesting years of all her glorious reign. There was great poetry about that time, and, it must be confessed, some peril.

Mrs. Oliphant, in her excellent little life of the Queen, says: "The immediate circle of friends around the young sovereign fed her with no flatteries."

It is difficult to believe such a statement of any mortal Court-circle. But if gross adulation was not offered—a sort of moral pabulum, which the Queen's admirable good sense would have rejected, there was profound homage in the very attitude of courtiers and in the etiquette of Court life. The incense of praise and admiration, "unuttered or exprest," was perpetually and inevitably rising up about her young footsteps wherever

35

they strayed; it formed the very air she breathed—about as healthful an atmosphere to live and sleep in as would be that of a conservatory abounding in tuberoses, white lilies, and jessamine.

Still, that she did not grow either arrogant or artificial, seems proved by the pleasant accounts given of her simple and gracious ways by the painters of whom I have spoken—Thomas Sully and Charles Leslie. I remember particularly, hearing from a friend of Mr. Sully, of the generous interest she took in his portrait of her, which, I think, was painted at Windsor. She gave him all the sittings, or rather standings, her busy life would allow; giving him free use of all the splendid paraphernalia necessary for his work. Between whiles the painter's young daughter stood for the picture, being, of course, obliged to don the royal robes and even the tiara. One day, while thus engaged and arrayed, the Queen came suddenly into the room. Miss Sully much confused was about to descend from the steps of the throne, when the Queen exclaimed, laughing: "Pray stay as you are; I like to see how I look!"

Leslie, whose picture of the Coronation was painted at Windsor, gave a pleasant account of the Queen's kindly and easy ways. "She is now," he says, "so far satisfied with the likeness that she does not wish me to touch it again. She sat five times—not only for the face, but for as much as is seen of the figure, and for the hands, with the coronation-ring on the finger. Her hands, by the by, are very pretty—the backs dimpled and the fingers delicately shaped. She was particular to have her hair dressed exactly as she wore it at the ceremony every time she sat."

The Queen in her writings says very little of this portion of her "strange, eventful history,"—a time so filled with incident, so gilded with romance, so bathed in poetry, so altogether splendid in the eyes of all the world; for to her, life—or all which was most "happy and glorious" in life—began and ended with Prince Albert. She even speaks with regret of that period of single queenliness, and says: "A worse school for a young girl—one more detrimental to all natural feelings and affections—cannot well be imagined than the position of a Queen at eighteen without experience and without a husband to guide and support her. This the Queen can state from painful experience, and she thanks God that none of her own dear daughters are exposed to such danger."

Human nature is rash and young-woman-nature ambitious and ill-disposed to profit by the costly experience of eld, and I doubt not the clever Princess Royal or the proud and fair Princess Louise would have mounted any throne in Christendom "without alarm." Most of Her Majesty's loyal subjects deny that any harm came to her from her unsupported position as Queen Regnant, or that she was capable of being thus harmed—but the Queen knows best.

The Princess Victoria was a proud, high-spirited girl, and it were no treason to suppose that at the first she had a sense of relief when the leading-strings, in which she had been so long held, were cut, though by the scissors of Atropos, and she was free to stand and go alone. Her good mother, becoming at once an object of political jealousy, removed herself from the old close companionship, though retaining in her heart the old tender solicitude—perhaps feeling herself more than ever necessary to her daughter. Mothers are so conceited. It is small wonder if after her life of studious and modest seclusion and filial subordination, the gaiety, the splendor, and the supremacy of the new existence intoxicated the young sovereign somewhat. The pleasures of her capital and the homage of the world captivated her imagination, while the consciousness of power and wealth and personal loveliness inclined her to be self-indulgent and self-willed. In spite of the good counsel of the family Mentor, Baron Stockmar, and of her sagacious uncle, Leopold, she must have committed some errors of judgment—fallen into some follies; she was so young and impulsive—so very human. Her first independent political act seems to have been a mistake, founded on a misunderstanding. It was at all events an act

36

more Georgian than Victorian. The Whig party, to which she was attached, had by a series of blunders and by weak vacillation lost strength and popularity, and Lord Melbourne's Ministry found itself so hard-pressed that it struck colors and resigned. Then the Queen was advised by the Duke of Wellington to invite the Conservative leader, Sir Robert Peel, to form a new Ministry. She did so, but frankly told that gentleman that she was very sorry to lose Lord Melbourne and his colleagues, whom she liked and approved—which must have been pleasant talk to Sir Robert. However, he went to work, but soon found that objections were made by his colleagues to certain Whig ladies in personal attendance on the Queen, and likely to influence her. So it was proposed to Her Majesty to make an important change in her household. I believe that the Duchess of Sutherland and Lady Normandy—the first the sister and the second the wife of a prominent Liberal—were especially meant; but the Queen took it that she was called on to dismiss all her ladies, and flatly refused, saying that to do so would be "repugnant to her feelings"—forgetting that feeling was no constitutional argument. She had got used to those Ladies of the Bed-Chamber, and they to her. They knew just where everything was, what colors became her, and what gossip and games amused her. Doubtless she loved them, and doubtless also she loved her own way. Surely the right of her constitutional advisers to dictate to her must have a limit somewhere, and she drew the line at her bed-chamber door. Then, as Sir Robert would not yield the point, she recalled Melbourne and went on as before. The affair created immense excitement. Non-political people were amused at the little Queen's spirit of independence. Liberals applauded her patriotism and pluck in defeating the "wicked Bed-Chamber Plot," and for her loyalty to her friends; but the defeated Tories were very naturally incensed, and, manlike, paid Her Majesty back, when measures which she had much at heart came before Parliament a year or so later—as we shall see.

Many years later the Queen appears to have thought that she was beginning to drift on to rocks of serious political mistakes and misfortunes as well as into rapids of frivolity, when the good, wise Pilot came to take the helm of her life-craft.

This pilot was, of course, the "Prince Charming," selected and reared for her away in Saxe-Coburg—that handsome Cousin Albert, once in a letter to the good uncle Leopold tacitly accepted by her in girlish thoughtlessness, as she would have accepted a partner in a joyous country-dance, and afterwards nearly as thoughtlessly thrown over and himself sent adrift.

CHAPTER XIV.

Prince Albert.

If the Princess Charlotte was the prototype of her cousin Victoria, Prince Leopold was in some respects the prototype of his beloved nephew Albert, who was born in August, 1819, at Rosenau, a charming summer residence of his father, the reigning Duke of Saxe-Coburg-Saalfield. The little Prince's grandmother, the Dowager-Duchess of Saxe-Coburg, in writing to her daughter, the Duchess of Kent, to announce the happy event, says: "The little boy is to be christened to-morrow, and to have the name of Albert."

When the christening came off it appeared that "Albert" was only one and the simplest of several names, but he was always known and always will be known by that name. It has been immortalized by his upright character, his rare intellectual gifts, his goodness and grace; by the affection of his countrymen and his noble life-work in England; by the genius of England's greatest living poet, and by the love and sorrow of England's Queen.

While the Prince was yet a baby, his mother wrote of him: "Albert is superb,— remarkably beautiful, with large blue eyes, a delicate mouth, a fine nose, and dimpled cheeks. He is lively and always gay."

Albert was the second son of the Duke and Duchess. Ernest, a year or two older, is thus described by his mother: "Ernest is very strong and robust, but not half so pretty as his brother. He is handsome, though; with black eyes."

Prince Leopold spent some time with his brother at Coburg when Albert was about two years old, and then began the tender, life-long mutual affection which led to such happy and important results. The young mother wrote: "Albert adores his uncle Leopold; never quits him for a moment; looks sweetly at him; is constantly embracing him; and is never happy except when near him."

The grandmother also wrote: "Leopold is very kind to the little boys. Bold *Albertinchen* drags him constantly about by the hand. The little fellow is the pendant to the pretty cousin (Princess Victoria); very handsome, but too slight for a boy; lively, very funny, all good nature, and full of mischief. The other day he did not know how to make enough of me, because I took him with me in the carriage. He kept saying, 'Albert is going with grandmamma!' and gave me his little hand to kiss. 'There, grandmamma, kiss!'"

The little Princes were not long to enjoy the care and society of their loving and lovely mother. An unhappy estrangement between their parents, followed by a separation and a divorce, left them at seven and five years old half-orphaned; for they never saw their mother again. She died at St. Wendel, in Switzerland, while still young and beautiful; but doubtless weary enough of life, which had brought her such happiness, only to take it away. Two words as holy as her prayers, were on her dying lips— "Ernest!" "Albert!"

But the boys were rich in grandmothers—having two of the very tenderest and dearest of Dowager-Duchesses to watch over them (watching each other, perhaps, the while) and to minister to them for many a year. According to these venerable ladies, Albert, who was certainly a delicate, nervous child, was one of those "little angels" who are destined not to survive the dimpled, golden-curled, lisping, and croupy period; being too good and sweet and exquisite for this wicked and rough world. But, according to certain entries in the Prince's own diary—his first, begun in his sixth year—he at that age happily revealed some hopeful signs of saving naughtiness and healthful "original sin."

"11th *February*, 1825. "I was told to recite something, but did not wish to do so. That was not right—naughty!"

"20th *February*. "I had left all my lesson books lying about in the room, and I had to put them away; then I cried."

"28th *February*.
"I cried at my lesson to-day because I could not find a verb, and the Rath (tutor) pinched me, to show me what a verb was. I cried about it."

"9th *April*. "I got up well and happy; afterward I had a fight with my brother."

"10th *April*. "I had another fight with my brother; that was not right."

This almost baby-prince seems to have been a valorous little fellow. When his blood was up he seems to have given little thought to the superior age or strength of his opponents, but to have been always ready to "pitch in"; or, to use the more refined and courtly language of his tutor, M. Florschütz, "he was not, at times, indisposed to resort to force, if his wishes were not at once complied with."

For several years the young Princes, devoted to each other, passed studious, yet active and merry lives at the Coburg Palace, and in the dear country home of Rosenau. They seem to have corresponded with their cousin Victoria, whom, it seems, the lad Albert was led by his grandmamma Coburg to regard with an especially romantic and tender interest. That grandmamma, the mother of Prince Leopold and the Duchess of Kent, and who seems to have been a very able and noble woman, died when her darling Albert was about twelve years old; but the hope of her heart did not die with her, and without doubt Prince Albert was educated with special and constant reference to a far more important

38

and brilliant destiny than often falls to the lot of the young sons of even Grand Ducal houses. He was well instructed in many branches of science, in languages, in music and literature, in politics, and what seems a contradiction, in ethics,— his moral development being most carefully watched over, while his physical training was a pendant to that which made his cousin Victoria one of the healthiest and hardiest of modern Englishwomen. With a delicate constitution and a sensitive, nervous temperament, Prince Albert would scarcely have lived to manhood, except for that admirable physical training. As a child, he was braced up by much life in the open air, simple diet, a good deal of rough play—while as to sleep, he was allowed to help himself, which he did plentifully, being much given to somnolency. As a lad and youth, he hardened himself by all healthful manly sports and exercises; in short, made a boy of mamma's "angel," a man of grandmamma's golden-haired darling. Nor was that great element of a liberal education, travel, wanting. The brothers paid visits to their uncle Leopold, now King of Belgium, and after tours in Germany, Austria, and Holland, visited England, and their aunt Kent and their cousin Victoria, to whom they were most warmly commended by their uncle.

According to the Queen's books, with this visit of three weeks began the personal acquaintance of the cousins; yet old Kensingtonians have a legend which they obstinately cling to, that Prince Albert, when much younger, spent three years in the old brick palace with his aunt and cousin, in pursuance of the matrimonial plans of the Duchess of Kent and Prince Leopold; and I have seen in a quaint old juvenile book a wood-cut representing the little Victoria in a big hat, riding on a pony in the park, and little Albert in a visored cap and short jacket running along at her side. But, of course, it was all a mistake; there was no such period of childish courtship, and the boy in the queer Dutch cap was an optical illusion, or a "double," in German a *doppel-gänger*. During the real visit, occurred the seventeenth birthday of the Princess, and there were public rejoicings and Court-festivities, preceded and followed for the cousins by days of pleasant companionship, in walking and riding, and evenings of music and dancing. But if the lad Albert, remembering the promise of his garrulous nurse, and the prophecy of his fond grandmamma, and the wish of his father and uncle Leopold, sought to read his destiny in the baffling blue eyes of the gay young girl, he seems to have failed, for he could only write home: "Our cousin is most amiable." Perhaps Victoria's own wonderful destiny, now drawing near, left little room in her heart or thought for lesser romances; perhaps the crown of England suspended over her head as by a single hair, the frail life of an old man, outdazzled even the graces and merits of her handsome but rather immature kinsman. Besides, "Prince Charming" at that time was short and stout, and he spoke our language too imperfectly to make love (which he would have pronounced *luf*) in the future Queen's English; and so he went away without any exchange of vows, or rings, or locks of fair hair or miniatures, and returned to his studies, principally at the University of Bonn. It is true that the Princess wrote to her "dearest uncle Leopold" soon after this visit, begging him to take special care of one now so dear to her, adding: "I hope and trust that all will go on prosperously and well on this subject now of so much importance to me." Yet King Leopold was a wise man, and did not build too securely on the fancy of a girl of seventeen, though he kept to work, he and the Baron, on their Prince-Consort making, in spite of the opposition of old King William, and all his brothers, and the candidates favored by them.

It was from quaint, quiet old Bonn that Prince Albert wrote, on his cousin's accession to the throne, his famous letter of congratulation, in which there appeared not one word of courtier-like adulation—not a thought calculated to stir the heart of the young girl suddenly raised to that giddy height overlooking the world, with a thrill of exultation or vain-gloriousness. Thus wrote this boy-man of eighteen: "Now you are Queen of the mightiest land of Europe; in your hand lies the happiness of millions. May Heaven assist you, and strengthen you with its strength in the high, but difficult task."

After leaving the University Prince Albert traveled in Switzerland and Italy with Baron Stockmar—everywhere winning the admiration and respect of the best sort of people by the rare princeliness of his appearance, his refined taste, his thoughtful and singularly receptive mind. And so three years went by. They were three years of uncertainty in regard to the great projects formed for him, of happiness, and a noble and useful, if subordinate career. King Leopold, the good genius of the two families, had not suffered his cousin to forget him, but though she declared she cared for no one else, she was not disposed to enter into any positive engagement, even with Albert. She enjoyed intensely her proud, independent position as Queen Regnant. She was having such a glorious swing at life, and very naturally feared the possible restraints, and the inevitable subordination of marriage. She was "too young to marry," and Albert was still younger—full three months. She would remain as she was, the gay, untrammeled maiden-Queen of England, for at least three or four years longer, and then think about it. The Prince was made, aware by his uncle Leopold of his royal cousin's state of feeling, or unfeeling, and was in a very doubtful and despondent state of mind when, polished by study and travel, grown tall and graceful, and "ideally beautiful," a veritable "Prince Charming," he came over the sea, out of fairyland, via Rotterdam, to seek his fortune—to attempt, at least, to wake the grandeur-enchanted Princess from her passionless dream of lonely, loveless sovereignty. He came, was seen, and conquered! But not at once; ah, no; for this charming royal idyll had its changing strophes, marking deepening degrees of sentiment—admiration, interest, hope, assurance, joyous certainty.

The Queen had resolved to receive both the Princes with cousinly affection and royal honors, but as though they had come on an ordinary visit. As for Albert, she meant probably to reason with him frankly, till he should be convinced that they were "ower young to marry yet"—till he should realize his own exceeding youthfulness. Then, as he must go away, and "wait a little longer," she would see as much of him as possible—he was such a good, constant fellow. But she must give due attention to her other guests; and then the State had some claim on her time. But when the Coburg Princes arrived at Windsor, and the Queen, with her mother, met them at the head of the grand staircase, somehow she had only eyes for the younger brother; he had grown so manly, so tall, quite out of the old objectionable stoutness; he had so improved in his English; he was so handsome—so every way presentable! So, in spite of the gaieties and forms, and the comings and goings of Windsor, so very much did the royal maiden, hitherto so gay and "fancy-free" see of her cousin Albert preparatory to bidding him an indefinite adieu, that on the second day even, cause for jealousy was given to aspiring courtiers by smiles and words, especially sweet and gracious, bestowed on the fair Saxon Knight. On that second day the Queen wrote to her uncle Leopold: "Albert's beauty is most striking, and he is most amiable and unaffected; in short, very fascinating." She then added, with an exquisite touch of maiden coyness: "The young men are *both* amiable, delightful companions, and I am glad to have them here."

When a few more days had passed in familiar intercourse, in singing and walking, in dancing and driving, and best of all, in riding together (for there is no cradle to rock young Love in like the saddle), the poor little Queen forsworn, found she had no longer the courage to propose to that proud young Prince to wait indefinitely on her will—to tarry at Coburg for more wisdom and beard. At the thought of it she seemed to see something of noble scorn about his lips, and such grave remonstrance in his gentle, pensive, forget-me-not eyes, that—the words of parting were never spoken, or not till after many happy years.

40

Alas for this fairy-Prince in an unfairylike kingdom! He could only declare his love, and sound the heart of his beloved, with his eyes. Etiquette put a leaden seal on his lips till from hers should come the sweet avowal and the momentous proffer to rule the ruler—to assume love's sovereignty over the Sovereign. After five days of troubled yet joyous waiting, it came—the happy "climax," as the Prince called it in a letter to Baron Stockmar—and then that perfectest flower of human life, whether in palace or cottage, a pure and noble love, burst into full and glorious bloom in each young heart. One cannot, even now, read without a genuine heart-thrill, and a mistiness about the eyes, the simple touching story of that royal romance of royal old Windsor. More than two-score years have passed, and yet how fresh it seems! It has the dew and the bloom of Paradise upon it.

What in all this story seems to me most beautiful and touching, because so exquisitely womanly, is the meekness of the young Queen. Though as Queen she offered the Prince her coveted hand—that hand that had held the sceptre of sceptres, and which Princes and Peers and the representatives of the highest powers on earth, had kissed in homage, it was only as a poor little woman's weak hand, which needed to be upheld and guided in good works, by a stronger, firmer hand; and her head, when she laid it on her chosen husband's shoulder, had not the feel of the crown on it. Indeed, she seems to have felt that his love was her real coronation, his faith her consecration.

To the beloved Stockmar, to whom but a little while before she had communicated her unalterable determination not to marry any one for ever so long the newly betrothed wrote: "I do feel so guilty I know not how to begin my letter; but I think the news it will contain will be sufficient to ensure your forgiveness. Albert has completely won my heart, and all was settled between us this morning. I feel certain he will make me happy. I wish I could feel as certain of my making him happy, but I will do my best."

Among the entries in the Queen's journal are many like this: "How I will strive to make Albert feel as little as possible the great sacrifice he has made. I told him it *was* a great sacrifice on his part, but he would not allow it."

Of course the Prince had too much manly feeling and practical good sense to "allow it." He knew he was the most envied, not only of all poor German Princes about that time, but of all young scions of royalty the world over; and besides, he loved his cousin. There is no record or legend or hint of his having ever loved any other woman, except his good grandmothers. To her of Gotha he wrote: "The Queen sent for me alone to her room the other day, and declared to me in a genuine outburst of affection that I had gained her whole heart, and would make me intensely happy if I would make her the sacrifice of sharing her life with her, for she said she looked on it as a sacrifice; the only thing which troubled her was that she did not think she was worthy of me. The joyous openness with which she told me this enchanted me, and I was quite carried away by it."

Still, and always the thought of "sacrifice!" This sentiment of tender humility, of deference and reverence the Queen never lost. Indeed, it seems to have grown with years, and as the character of the Prince- Consort unfolded more and more in beauty, strength, dignity, and uprightness.

A month was passed by the lovers, in such happiness as comes but once in life to the most fortunate human beings—to some, alas! never. Then the Prince returned to Coburg, to settle his affairs and to take leave of his old home and his kindred. Those partings seem to have pulled hard on his heart-strings, and are distressing to read about. One would think he was bound for the "under-world," to wed the Queen of Madagascar. These Germans are such passionate lovers of the fatherland, that one wonders how they can ever bring themselves to leave it, to make grand marriages in England, or fortunes in America, to start a royal house, or a kindergarten—to become a Field Marshal or a United States Senator.

41

But all that grief at Coburg and Gotha showed how dearly Prince Albert was loved, and how he loved.

It seems that the fair cousin at Windsor was scarcely gay, for the Prince, writing to her mother, says: "What you say of my poor little bride, sitting all alone in her room, silent and sad, has touched my heart. Oh, that I might fly to her side to cheer her!"

But she could not have much indulged in this solitary, idle brooding, for she had work to do, and must be up and doing. First, she had to summon a Privy Council, which met at Buckingham Palace;—more than eighty Peers, mostly solemn old fellows, who had outlived their days of romantic sentiment, if they ever had any, yet to whom the Queen had to declare her love for her cousin Albert, and her intention to marry him, being convinced, she said, that this union would "secure her domestic felicity, and serve the interests of her country." It was a little hard, yet a certain bracelet, containing a certain miniature, which she wore on her arm, gave her "courage," she said. Then came a yet more trying ordeal, for a modest young lady—the announcement of her intended marriage, in a speech from the throne, in the House of Lords. With the utmost dignity and calmness, and with a happiness which sparkled in her eyes and glowed in her blushes, and made strangely beautiful her young face, she read the announcement in the clear, musical tones so peculiar to her, and with an, almost religious solemnity. The glory of pure maidenly trust and devotion resting on her head, outshone the jewels of her tiara; Love was enthroned at her side.

All was not sunshine, rose-bloom and soft airs before the young German husband of the Queen. Much doubt and jealousy and some unfriendliness were waiting for him in high places. The disappointed Tory party, and some Radicals, opposed hotly the proposed grant for the Prince of £50,000, and at last cut it down to £30,000.

Then came a discussion over a clause in the Bill for the Naturalization of the Prince, empowering the husband of the Queen to take precedence over even the Royal Princes, and to be ever at her side, where he belonged, which, though finally assented to by these most interested in England—the Dukes of Sussex and Cambridge—was stoutly opposed by their elder brother, the Duke of Cumberland, for Heaven and Hanover had not relieved the English Government of "the bogie." In support of his rights, Wellington and Brougham stood out, and the clause was dropped. But the Queen, by the exercise of her prerogative, gave the Prince the title of Royal Highness, and made him a Field Marshal in the British army; and about a month later, she settled the precedence question, as far as concerned England, by proclaiming that by her royal will and pleasure her husband should "enjoy place, pre-eminence and precedence, next to Her Majesty."

The amiable Prince is said never to have cherished resentment towards Sir Robert Peel and others who had voted to cut down his allowance, or the Duke of Wellington, and Lord Brougham, who had argued that those tiresome old gentlemen, the Royal Dukes, should have the right to walk and sit next to *his* wife on State occasions; but Victoria confesses that she long felt "most indignant." She was hurt not only in her wifely love, but in her queenly pride.

Greville says of Kings: "The contrast between their apparent authority and the contradictions which they practically meet with, must be peculiarly galling—more especially to men whose minds are seldom regulated by the beneficial discipline of education, and early collision with their equals." It must be yet more "galling" for Queens, because they always have been more flattered, and are imaginative enough to fancy that in grasping the symbols they hold the power.

But I do not believe that the royal lovers took deeply to heart these disagreeable matters at this time. I hope they didn't mourn much over the £20,000 they didn't get. I hope that Love lifted them far above the murky air of party strife and petty jealousy into a clear, serene atmosphere of its own. They knew—and it was a great thing to know—that they had the sympathy of all the true hearts of the realm, whether beating under the "purple and fine linen" of the rich and noble, or the rough and simple garments of the poor and humble.

On the 10th of February, 1840, Prince Albert, always tenderly thoughtful of the dear old Dowager of Saxe-Gotha, his "*liebe grosmama*" who, when he had parted from her last, had stood at her window, weeping, stretching out her arms and so desolately calling after him, "Albert! Albert!" sat down and wrote as no beautifulest Prince of poetry or romance ever wrote to a feeble, old female relative on his wedding-day:

"DEAR GRANDMAMMA: In less than three hours, I shall stand at the altar, with my dear bride. In these solemn moments, I must once more ask your blessing, which I am well assured I shall receive, and which will be my safeguard and future joy. I must end. God be my stay!

"Your faithful

"ALBERT."

This letter may seem a little too solemn and ill-assured, but it shows in what a serious and devout spirit this young Prince, not yet of age, entered on that auspicious and splendid union, whose wedding-bells rang round the world. Moreover, the young man's position was a rather trying one. As yet, he was little known in England, while it was well known that the Royal Family had been from the first opposed to his marriage with Victoria. Though the land of the Teutons had so long been the nursery of English Kings and Queens, the English common people were jealous of Teutonic Princes—regarding them for the most part as needy adventurers, for whom England was only the great milch-cow of Germany. Prince Albert had a host of prejudices to live down; and he did live down most of them, but some have died hard over his grave.

The Queen's wedding was second only to the coronation, as a grand and beautiful pageant for the privileged few who could witness it, for of course the old Royal Chapel of St. James was a much narrower stage for the great scene than the Abbey. Still, royalty and nobility turned out in force, and all the greatest of the great were there. The sombre chapel was made to look very gay and gorgeous with hangings and decorations; even before the ladies in rich dresses and with all their costliest jewels on, and the gentlemen in brilliant uniforms and Court-costumes arrived. The bridegroom, when he walked up the aisle, between his father and his brother, bowing affably right and left, drew forth murmurs of admiration by his rare beauty and grace—princeliest of Princes.

The Queen is described as looking unusually pale, but very lovely, in a magnificent robe of lace over white satin trimmed with orange blossoms, and with a most exquisite Honiton veil. In the midst of her twelve bridesmaids, her face radiant with happiness, she seemed like the whitest of diamonds set in pearls—or so they say.

Her Majesty is also described as bearing herself with great dignity and composure, and to have gone through the service very solemnly. And yet I have heard a little story that runs thus: When Prince Albert, in this last act of "*Le Jeune Homme Pauvre*" came to repeat, as he placed the ring on her finger, the words, "With all my worldly goods I thee endow," the merry girl-Queen was unable to suppress an arch smile.

The Duchess of Kent is described as looking "tearful and distressed." Ah, why will mothers always cry at their daughters' weddings, even when they have hoped and schemed for that very match; and why will brides, though ever so much in love, weep, first or last, on the wedding morning? Lady Lyttleton, in her correspondence, said of the Queen—"Her eyes were swollen with tears; but," she adds, "there was great happiness in her countenance, and her look of confidence and comfort at the Prince, when they walked away, as man and wife, was very pleasant to see."

43

Ah, "when they walked away as man and wife"—now simply and for always to each other, "Albert" and "Victoria," the separate life of our "Prince Charming" closed. Thenceforth, the two bright life-streams seemed to flow on together, completely merged, indistinguishable, indivisible, but only *seemed*—for, alas, one has reached the great ocean before the other.

PART III.

WIFEHOOD AND MOTHERHOOD.

CHAPTER XV.

The first months of Marriage—Incidents and anecdotes—The adoption of Penny postage—The Inauguration of Steam Railway travel—The Duchess of Kent takes a separate residence—Prince Albert presides at a meeting favoring the abolition of the Slave Trade.

In this mere sketch of the great life of the Queen of England, I can give little space to the political questions and events of her reign, important and momentous as some of them were, even for other lands and other people than the English. For a clear and concise account of those questions and events, I refer my readers to "A History of Our Own Times," by Justin McCarthy, M.P. I know nothing so admirable of its kind. But mine must be something less ambitious—a personal and domestic history— light, gossipy, superficial, as regards the profound mysteries of politics; in short, "pure womanly."

I shall not even treat of the great wars which stormed over the Continent, and upset and set up thrones, except as they affected the life of my illustrious subject. At first they seemed to form a lurid background to the bright pictures of peace and love presented by her happy marriage and maternity, and afterwards in the desolation and mourning they brought, seemed in keeping with the sorrow of her widowhood.

Happily all was quiet and peace in the United Kingdom, and in the world at large, when the honeymoon began for that august but simple-hearted pair of lovers, Victoria and Albert; or, as she would have preferred to write it, Albert and Victoria. The fiery little spurt of revolt in Canada, called rather ambitiously, "The Canadian Rebellion," had ended in smoke, and the outburst of Chartism, from the spontaneous combustion of sullen and long-smothered discontent among the working classes, had been extinguished, partly by a fog of misapprehension and misdirection, partly by a process of energetic stamping out. The shameful Chinese opium war, the Cabul disasters, and the fearful Sepoy rebellion were, as yet, only slow, simmering horrors in the black caldron of the Fates. Irish starvation had not set in, in its acute form, and Irish sedition was, as yet, taking only the form of words—the bold, eloquent, magnificent, but not malignant and scarcely menacing words of Daniel O'Connell In the Infernal Council Chamber below, the clock whose hours are epochs of crime, had not yet struck for the era of political assassination. France was resting and cooling from the throes and fires of revolution, and growing the vine over its old lava courses. The citizen-King and his family were setting an example of domestic affection and union, of morality, thrift, and forehandedness—diligently making hay while the fickle sun of French loyalty was shining. Italy was lying deathly quiet under the mailed foot of Austria, and under the paternal foot of the old Pope, shod with a velvet slipper, cross-embroidered, but leaden-soled; Garibaldi was fighting for liberty in "the golden South Americas"; Mazzini was yet dreaming of liberty—so was Kossuth. Russia was quietly gathering herself up for new leaps of conquest tinder her most imperial, inflexible autocrat—the inscrutable, unsmiling Nicholas.

In England and America it was, though a peaceful, a stirring and an eventful time. English manufacturers, not content with leveling mountains of American cotton bales, converting them into textile fabrics and clothing the world therewith, were reaching deep and deeper into the bowels of the earth, and pulling up sterner stuff to spin into gigantic threads with which to lace together all the provinces and cities of the realm. That captive monster, Steam, though in the early days of its servitude, was working well in harness, while in America Morse was after the lightning, lassoing it with his galvanic wires. In England the steam- dragon had begun by killing one of his keepers, and was distrusted by most English people, who still preferred post-horses and stage-coaches— all the good old ways beloved by hostel-keepers, Tony Welters, postilions and pot-boys. There was something fearful, supernatural, almost profane and Providence-defying in this new, swift, wild, and whizzing mode of conveyance. Churchmen and Tories were especially set against it; yet I have been told that later, that Prince of conservatives, F. M., the Duke of Wellington, did, on the occasion of one of Her Majesty's *accouchements* travel from London to Windsor, at the rate of seventy-five miles an hour, in order to be in at the birth! What were the perils of Waterloo to this daring, dizzying journey?

Just a month before the Queen's marriage there occurred in London a union yet more auspicious, not alone for England, but for all Christendom. It was the wedding, by act of Parliament, of Knowledge and Humanity in the cheap postage reform—carried through with wonderful ability, energy, persistence, and pluck by Rowland Hill; blessed be his memory. The Queen afterwards knighted him, but he did not need the honor, though I doubt not it was pleasant, coming from her hands. The simple name of the dear old man was full of dignity, and long before had been stamped—penny- stamped, on the heart of the world.

So it seemed that life smiled on and around the royal wedded pair on that winter afternoon, so unwintry to them, when they took leave of relations and wedding guests at Buckingham Palace, and set out for Windsor Castle. Even the heavens which had wept in the morning with those who wept, changed its mood, and smiled on bride and bridegroom, as they drove forth in an open carriage and four, followed by other open carriages containing a picked suite of friends and attendants—all with favor-decked postilions and footmen in the royal red liveries, and everything grand and gay. The Queen was dressed in a white satin *pelisse*, profusely trimmed with swan's-down. She seems, in those days, to have been very fond of nestling down under that soft, warm, dainty sort of a wrap. How like a white dove she must have looked that day, for her bonnet was white, trimmed with white, plumes. Prince Albert wore a fur-trimmed coat, with a high collar, and had a very high hat, which for the most part was in his hand, so much saluting was he obliged to do to the saluting multitude.

All the world was abroad that day—great was the flow of good feeling, and mighty was the flow of good ale, while the whole air of the Kingdom was vibrating with the peal of merry marriage-bells. All through the land free dinners were provided for the poor—good roast beef, plum-pudding— 'alf and 'alf fare—and I am afraid the Queen's pauper-subjects would have been unwilling to have the occasion indefinitely repeated, with such observances,—would not have objected to Her Majesty proving a female Henry VIII.

Victoria and Albert drove that afternoon more than twenty miles between ranks of frantically loyal, rejoicing people,—past countless festive decorations, and a world of "*V*"s and "*A*"s—under arches so gay that one wondered where and how at that season all the flowers and foliage were produced,—if nature had not hurried up her spring work, so as to be able to come to the wedding. The Queen turned now and then her happy face on her shouting subjects, in graceful acknowledgment of their sympathy with her happiness; but much of the time she was observed to be regarding her husband, intently or furtively. So she had betrayed her heart during She marriage ceremony, when, as an eye-witness records, she "was observed to look frequently at Prince Albert,—in fact, she scarcely ever took her eyes off him." I suppose she found him "goodly to look upon." It is certain that she worshiped him with her eyes, as well as with her heart and soul,—then and ever after. For the world, even for the Court, he grew, as the pitiless, pilfering years went by, a little too stout, and somewhat bald, while his complexion lost something of its fine coloring and smoothness, and his eyes their fulness,—but for her, he seems to have always kept the grace and glory of his youth. Even when he was dying-when the gray twilight of the fast-coming night was creeping over his face, clouding the light of his eyes, chilling the glow of his smile—his beauty was still undimmed for her. She says in her pathetic account of those sad moments—"his beautiful face, more beautiful than ever, is grown so thin."

But on this their wedding-day, death and death-bed partings were far enough from the thoughts of the royal lovers. Life was theirs,—young life, in all its fulness and richness of health, and hope, and joy, and that "perfect, love, which casteth out fear."

So essentially young and so light-hearted were they, that they laughingly welcomed the crowd of shouting, leaping, hat-waving, mad Eton boys, who as they neared Windsor, turned out to receive them. The Queen jotted down this jolly incident in her journal thus: "The boys in a body accompanied the carriage to the castle, cheering and shouting as only schoolboys can. They swarmed up the mound, as the carriage entered the quadrangle, and, as the Queen and the Prince descended at the grand entrance, they made the old castle ring again with their acclamations."

What would Queen Charlotte, or any of the stiff, formal Dutch Queens of any of the Georges have thought of such a boisterous wedding escort,—of such a noisy welcome to stately Windsor? They would very likely have said, "Go away, naughty *pays*! How dare you!"

Alas, this royal pair, natural, joyous, girl-like and boy-like as they were still were slaves to, their station. They could not long hide themselves from the million-eyed world. In a few days the Court came down upon them from London. "Mamma" came with them—and I hope that she, at least, was welcome. Then followed show and ceremony, and amusements of the common, unpoetic, unparadisiacal, Courtly order. There were "fiddling and dancing every night," and feasting, and full-dressing, and all that. Still nothing seems to have interfered much with the Queen's happiness and content, for Lady Lyttleton wrote of her about this time,—"I understand she is in extremely high spirits. Such a new thing for her to dare to be unguarded in conversing with anybody, and with her frank and fearless nature, the restraints she has hitherto been under, from one reason or another, with everybody, must have been most painful."

Only the day after her marriage, the Queen wrote to Baron Stockmar: "There cannot exist a purer, dearer, nobler being in the world than the Prince."

She never took those words back—she never had cause to take them back, to lie heavy on her heart. But such utter adoration persisted in year after year, with cheerful obstinacy, even against the modest protests of the object, would have spoiled any man who was spoilable.

Her Majesty was soon obliged to return to London, in order to hold Courts, to receive addresses of congratulation on her marriage. It seemed that half the men of the Kingdom of any standing, had formed themselves into delegations. So numerous were they, that Prince Albert was obliged to "come up to the help of the QUEEN against the mighty"— bore, for she records that he in one day received and personally answered no less than twenty-seven addresses! In fact, he was nearly addressed to death.

The Queen after receiving many members of both Houses of Parliament, bearing addresses—received large delegations from the State Church—the General Assembly of the Church of Scotland—the English Non-Conformists, and the Society of Friends—all walking peacefully enough together to the throne of Victoria, but having widely different ways to the "throne of grace;"—all uniting in loyal prayers for the divine blessing on the fair head of their Sovereign, and in the hope that the comely young man of her choice might do virtuously, and walk humbly, and gingerly by her side— but a little in the rear, as became him; not, of course, as a husband, Scripturally regarded, but as the German Consort of an English Queen *regnant*.

This subordinate view of her husband's place the Queen did not fully accept from anybody, at any time. At that period, it is probable she would have gladly taken off the crown, to place it on his dear head, and doffed the ermine mantle to put it on his manly shoulders, and would have been the first to swear allegiance to "King Albert."

She thought that he might, at least, have the title of "King-Consort," and perhaps because of this hope, she deferred for years—till 1857— conferring on him, by Royal Letters Patent, the title of Prince-Consort.

Doubtless the English people, if they had been on the lookout for a King, might have gone farther and fared worse,—but the four Georges had somehow got them out of conceit with the word "King," and William, the Sailor, had not quite reconciled them to it;—then they were jealous of foreigners, and last, but not least, there were apprehensions that the larger title would necessitate a larger grant. But the Prince did not need the empty honor, which in his position would have been "a distinction without a difference." I do not believe he cared much for it, though titles are usually dear to the Teutonic soul, determined, as he always so wisely was, to "sink his individuality in that of the Queen," and when at last, the second best title of Prince-Consort, that by which the people already named him, was made his legal right, by his fond wife, grieved to have kept

—"the best man under the sun, So many years from his due,"

he was well content, because it pleased her.

The Queen certainly did all she constitutionally could to confer honors on her husband, who after all outdid her, and best honored himself.

Before their marriage, she had invested him with the noble order of the Garter, and given him the Star, and the Badge, and the Garter itself set in diamonds. She now invested him with the insignia of a Knight Grand Cross of the Order of the Bath. It amused her, this investing—she would have liked to invent a few orders, for royal Albert's sake—he became the insignia so well! She also made him Colonel of the 11th Regiment of Light Dragoons—he rode so well!—and she had the name changed to "Prince Albert's Own Hussars."

Everywhere the Queen and Prince appeared together—at reviews and art exhibitions, at church and at the theatre (for the Queen was very fond of the drama in those days), at drawing-rooms and at races—and everywhere the people delighted in their beauty and their happiness.

Early in April, the Duchess of Kent, in pursuance of what she deemed her duty, and best for the young people, parted from her darling daughter, and took up her residence in a separate home in London—Ingestrie House. She afterwards occupied Clarence House, the present residence of the Duke of Edinburgh. When the Court was at Windsor, the Duchess resided at Frogmore, a very lovely place, belonging to the royal estate, and so near the Castle that she was able to dine and lunch with Victoria almost daily. Still the partial separation was a trial for a mother and daughter so closely and tenderly attached, and they both took it hard,—as did, about that time, Prince Albert his separation from his brother Ernest, whose long visit was over. The Queen's account of the exceeding sorrowfulness of that parting must now bring to the lips of the most sentimental reader, though "a man and a brother," an unsympathetic smile— unless he happens to remember that those were the earliest days of steam on sea and land, and that journeys from England to any part of the Continent were no light undertakings. So the brothers sung together a mournful college song, and embraced, kissing one another on both cheeks,

47

doubtless, after the German fashion,—"poor Albert being pale as a sheet, and his eyes full of tears." Ah, what would he have said could his "prophetic soul" have beheld his son, Albert Edward, skipping from London to Paris in eight hours—dashing about the Continent, from Copenhagen to Cannes, from Brussels to Berlin—from Homburg to St. Petersburg—taking it all as lightly and gaily as a school-boy takes a "jolly lark" of a holiday trip to Brighton or Margate! That was not the day of peregrinating Princes. Now they are as plenty as commercial travelers.

Early in June the Queen and Prince and their Court left busy, smoky London for a few days of quiet and pure air at lovely Claremont. They spent part of that restful time in going to the Derby, in four carriages and four with outriders and postilions—a brave sight to see.

On the first of June, Prince Albert was invited to preside at a great public meeting in Exeter Hall, for the abolition of the Slave Trade—and he did preside, and made a good speech, which he had practiced over to the Queen in the morning. That was an ordeal, for he spoke in English for the first time, and before a very large and distinguished audience. It was a very young "Daniel come to judgment" on an ancient wrong—for the Prince was not yet of age.

That sweet Quakeress, Caroline Fox, thus speaks of the Prince on this interesting occasion, in her delightful "Memories":—"Prince Albert was received with tremendous applause, but bore his honors with calm and modest dignity. He is certainly a very beautiful man,—a thorough German, and a fine poetical specimen of the race."

Ah, what would that doughty champion of the Slave Trade, William IV., have said, could he have seen his niece's husband giving royal countenance to such a fanatical, radical gathering! It was enough to make him stir irefully in his coffin at Windsor.

But for that matter, could our ancestors generally, men and women who devoutly believed in the past, and died in the odor of antiquity, know of our modern goings-on, in political and humanitarian reforms—know of our "Science so called," and social ethics, there would be "a rattling among the dry bones," not only in royal vaults, but in country churchyards, where *The rude forefathers of the hamlet sleep."*

CHAPTER XVI.

Death passes by—Life comes.

On the 10th of June, 1840, occurred the first mad attempt to assassinate Queen Victoria—made as she and Prince Albert were driving up Constitution Hill, near Buckingham Palace, in a small open phaeton. Prince Albert, in a letter to his grandmamma, gives the clearest account of it. He says: "We had hardly proceeded a hundred yards from the Palace, when I noticed, on the foot-path on my side, a little, mean-looking man, holding something toward us, and, before I could distinguish what it was, a shot was fired, which almost stunned us both, it was so loud—barely six paces from us. ... The horses started, and the carriage stopped. I seized Victoria's hands and asked if the fright, had not shaken her, but she laughed."

Almost immediately the fellow fired a second shot, from which the Queen was saved probably by the presence of mind of the Prince, who drew her down beside him. He states that the ball must have passed just over her head. The wretch was at once arrested and taken away, and soon after committed for trial, on the charge of high treason. The Queen was seen to be very pale, but calm. She rose in the carriage to show the excited people that she was not hurt, and then ordered the postilions to drive at once to Ingestrie House, that the Duchess of Kent might hear of the startling incident first from her and not be frightened by wild rumors. It was a thoughtful and filial act, and brave, moreover, for there were those about her who suspected that there might be a revolutionary conspiracy, and that Oxford was only one of many banded assassins. These alarmists advised her and her husband to show themselves abroad as little as possible. How they heeded this advice is shown in another passage of Prince Albert's letter: "We arrived safely at Aunt Kent's. From thence we took a drive through the Park, to give Victoria a little air,—also to show the people that we had not, on account of what had happened, lost confidence in them."

The Prince does not mention a very pretty incident which I find recorded elsewhere. As the Queen's carriage reached the Park, it was received with enthusiastic cheers, smiles, and tears by crowds of people, equestrians and pedestrians, and the gay world on wheels; and as they neared the Marble Arch, the gentlemen and ladies on horseback followed them as with one impulse—all Rotton Row turned out, and escorted them to Buckingham Palace. It is said, too, that for several days this was repeated—that whenever the Queen and Prince drove out they were escorted by this singular volunteer body-guard.

Of course, the whole country was excited, and the Queen, whose life had been menaced, was more popular than ever. They say that her first visit to the opera after this shocking attempt was a most memorable occasion. Her reception was something almost overwhelming. The audience were all on their feet, cheering and shouting, and waving handkerchiefs and hats, and there was no quieting them till the National Anthem was sung—and even then, they broke in with wild cheers at the close of every verse. Her Majesty stood throughout these demonstrations, bowing and smiling, her heart melted within her, I doubt not.

Of course there was no conspiracy, and Oxford the pot-boy, "a pot-boy was, and, nothing more." He was acquitted on the ground of insanity, but ordered to be confined "during Her Majesty's pleasure," which he was in Bedlam for some years. Then he was sent to Australia as cured, and where he went into better business than shooting Queens, and earned an honest living, they say. He always declared that he was not insane, except from a mad passion for notoriety—which he got.

The five or six successors of Oxford who have shot at Her Majesty, and that wretched retired officer, Robert Pate, who waylaid her in 1850, and struck her a cruel blow across the face with a walking-stick, were pronounced insane, and confined in mad-houses merely. The English are too proud and politic to admit that a sane man can lift his hand against the Constitutional Sovereign of England. When there arrived in London the news of the shooting of President Garfield, a distinguished English gentleman said to me, "I think we will not be annexed to the United States while you shoot your Presidents."

I replied by reminding him of the many attempts on the life of his beloved Queen, adding, "I believe the homicidal mania is a Monarchical as well as a Republican affliction,—the difference only is that, unhappily for us, our madmen are the better shots."

It must be that for monarchists born and bred, an anointed head, whether covered by a silk hat or a straw bonnet, is circled by a *simulacrum* of a crown, which dazzles the aim of the would-be regicide, they are so almost certain to miss, at long or short range. Alas there is no halo of sovereignty or "hedge of divinity" about our poor Presidents! It is, perhaps, because of this unsteadiness of nerve and aim, that Continental regicides are taking to sterner and surer means—believing that no thrice blessed crown can dazzle off dynamite, and that no most imperial "divinity" is bomb-proof.

In July an act which was the shadow of a coming event, was passed by Parliament, and received the Royal assent. It provided that Prince Albert should be Regent in case that the Queen should die before her next lineal descendant should attain the age of eighteen years.

In August the Queen prorogued Parliament for the first time since her marriage, and she brought her handsome husband to show to all the Lords and gentlemen—bravely attired in his Field-Marshal's uniform, with his Collars of the Garter and the Bath, and diamond

Stars—and she had him seated only a little lower than herself and very near, in a splendid chair, gilded, carved, and velvet-cushioned. The Prince wrote to his father as a piece of good news, "The prorogation of Parliament passed off very quietly." He had had reason to fear that his right to sit in that lofty seat would be disputed—that the old Duke of Sussex might come hobbling up to the throne, calling out, "I object! I object!"

But nothing of the kind happened. The Queen, by her wit and her courage, had circumvented all the royal old sticklers for precedence—who put etiquette before nature. The Queen's mother, and her uncle and aunt, the King and Queen of Belgium, were present,—so it was quite a family-party. The good Uncle Leopold was observed to smile benignly on both Victoria and Albert, as though well pleased with his work. The Queen was most magnificently attired with all her glories on, in the shape of diamonds and orders, and looked very proud and happy,—and yet there was a dreamy, half-troubled expression in her eyes at times, which was not usual, but which her mother understood.

On this day, Prince Albert's *status* was fixed. He had taken a ride with his wife, in the State-carriage, with the twelve cream-colored, long-tailed State horses, and the gorgeous footmen, and he had sat higher, and nearer the throne than any other man in the House of Lords, Prince or Peer. The next thing the Queen did for him was to make him a member of the Privy Council. But a little later, he had a higher promotion than that; for, on the 21st of November, the Princess Royal was born in Buckingham Palace, in the early afternoon.

During the morning the Duchess of Kent had been sent for—and came hurrying over. They also sent for the Duke of Sussex, the Archbishop of Canterbury, the Bishop of London, the Lord Chancellor, Lord Melbourne, Lord Palmerston, Lord Errol, Lord Albemarle—Lord John Russell, and other Privy Councillors, whose constitutional duty it is to be present at the birth of an heir to the throne of England,—and they came bustling in, as old ladies come together on a like occasion in country places in New England. It is probable they all looked for a boy. The girl was an extraordinary baby, however, for when she was barely two days old, her papa wrote to her grandpapa at Coburg, "The little one is very well and very merry." The Prince welcomed her in a fatherly way, though, as he confesses, sorry that she was the same sort of a human creature as her mother,—that is, a daughter instead of a son. He wrote to his father very frankly, "I should certainly have liked it better if she had been a son, as would Victoria also," and so, strangely enough, would the English people—unfortunate as they had often been with their Kings, and fortunate as they had always been with their Queens. The great officers of the Church and State went away probably saying, "Only a girl!" Dear "little Pussie," as she was often called, wouldn't have been so "merry" if she had known how it was. She was looked upon as a temporary stop-gap- -something to keep out Cumberland, and naturally she did not have so many silver cups and gold spoons as she would have had if she had been a boy— nor so many guns, poor thing! When the firing ceased at the feminine limit, people all over the city said, "Only a girl!"

Some years later, when, at the birth of one of her brothers, the guns were booming away, Douglas Jerrold exclaimed to a friend at dinner: "How they do powder these royal babies!"

The Queen in her journal gives a beautiful account of her husband's devotion to her during her illness. She says, always speaking of herself in the third person: "During the time the Queen was laid up, his care and devotion were quite beyond expression. He refused to go to the play, or anywhere else; generally dining alone with the Duchess of Kent, till the Queen was able to join them, and was always on hand to do anything in his power for her comfort. He was content to sit by her in a darkened room, to read to her or write for her. No one but himself ever lifted her from her bed to her sofa, and he always helped to wheel her on her sofa into the next room. For this purpose he would come

50

instantly when sent for from any part of the house. As years went on, and he became overwhelmed with work, this was often done at much inconvenience to himself (for his attentions were the same in all the Queen's subsequent confinements), but he always came with a sweet smile on his face. In short," the Queen adds, "his care of her was like that of a mother, nor could there be a kinder, wiser, or more judicious nurse."

The Prince also during the Queen's illness, conferred with her ministers, and transacted all necessary business for her. There were nine of these natural illnesses. I commend the example of the Prince-Consort to the husbands of America, to husbands all over the world.

It was a glad and grateful Christmas which they spent in Windsor that year—the first after their marriage,—the first since their union, so pompously and piously blessed by priests and people, had been visibly blessed by Heaven.

The next month the Queen opened Parliament in person, and gave the Lords and gentlemen another elocutionary treat in her admirable reading of her speech,—that "most excellent thing in woman," a sweet voice, telling even on the Tories. Prince Albert was with her, of course, and she looked even prouder and happier than usual. She had found yet new honors for herself and for him,—the most noble and ancient orders of Maternity and Paternity,—exceeding old, and yet always new.

That day the young Prince may have felt glowing in his heart a sweet prescience of the peculiar comfort and joy he afterwards found in the loving devotion and noble character of his firstborn, that little blessing that *would* come, though "only a girl."

That day the Queen wore in her diadem a new jewel, a "pearl of great price,"—a pure little human soul.

That faithful stand-by, King Leopold, came over to stand as chief sponsor at the christening of the Princess Royal,—which took place at Buckingham Palace, on the anniversary of her mother's marriage. The little girl, who received the names of Victoria Adelaide Mary Louisa, is said by her father to have behaved "with great propriety and like a Christian."

So ended the first year of Queen Victoria's married life. To say it had been a happy year would seem, after the records we have, to put a very inadequate estimate on its degree of harmony and content—and yet it were much to say of any marriage, during the trying period in which many of the tastes and habits of two separate lives must be harmonized, and some heroically abandoned. It is a period of readjustment and sacrifice. Redundant and interfering growths of character must be pruned away, and yet if the lopping process is carried too far, character itself must suffer, the juices of its life and power, individuality and will, are wasted.

The Queen always contended that it was the Prince who made all the sacrifices—unselfishly adjusting his life and character to suit hers, and her position—yet not long after her marriage she records the fact that she was beginning to sympathize with him in his peculiar tastes, particularly in his love for a quiet country life. She says: "I told Albert that formerly I was too happy to go to London, and wretched to leave it; and now since the blessed hour of my marriage, and still more since the summer, I dislike and am unhappy to leave the country, and could be content and happy never to go to town. This pleased him."

I am afraid that there are those of Her Majesty's subjects who bless not the memory of "Albert the Good," for this metamorphose of their once gay and thoughtless, ball-giving, riding, driving, play-going Queen. These malcontents are Londoners proper, mostly tradesmen, newspaper men, milliners, and Hyde Park idlers. I think American visitors and Cook's tourists are among those who hold that the Queen's proper place is in her capital—at least during the season while *they* are here.

51

Upon the whole, I should say of that first year of Queen Victoria's married life, that the honeymoon lasted throughout those twelve bright and busy (perhaps bright because busy) months. Or, it would seem that some fairy Godmother had come to that wedding, in homely guise, bringing as her humble gift, a jar of honey—but a miraculous jar, the honey gathered from Arcadian flowers, and which perpetually renewed itself, like the poor widow's blessed cruse of oil.

CHAPTER XVII.

The Boy "Jones" and his singular pranks—A change in the Ministry—Sir Robert Peel becomes Premier—Prince Albert made Chairman of the Fine Arts Commission—Birth of the Prince of Wales—The Queen commemorates the event by a beautiful act.

The next sensation in connection with the Court was the discovery of the famous "boy Jones" in Buckingham Palace. This singular young personage was by no means a stranger in the Palace. He had made himself very familiar with, and at home in that august mansion, about two years before. He was then arrested, and had lived an exceedingly retired life ever since. On that first occasion he was discovered by one of the porters, very early one morning, leisurely surveying one of the apartments. He was caught and searched; nothing of any consequence was found on him, but in a hall was a bundle, evidently made up by him, containing such incongruous articles as old letters, a sword, and a pot of bear's grease. He he appearance of a sweep, being very sooty, but disclaimed the chimney-cleaning profession. He had occupied, for a while, the vacant room of one of the Equerries, leaving in the bed the impress of his sooty figure. He declared that he had not entered the Palace for the purpose of theft, but only to gratify his curiosity, as to how royal people and "great swells" like royal footmen, lived. The young rascal's examination before the Magistrate caused much amusement. In answer to questions, he admitted, or boasted that he had been in the Palace previously, and for days at a time—in fact, had "put up" there—adding, "And a very comfortable place I found it. I used to hide behind the furniture and up the chimneys, in the day-time; when night came, I walked about, went into the kitchen, and got my food, I have seen the Queen and her ministers in Council, and heard all they had to say."

Magistrate: "Do you mean to say you have worn but one shirt all the time?"

Prisoner: "Yes; when it was dirty, I washed it out in the kitchen. The apartment I like best is the drawing-room."

Magistrate: "You are a sweep, are you?"

Prisoner: "Oh, no; it's only my face and hands that are dirty; that's from sleeping in the chimneys.... I know my way all over the Palace, and have been all over it, the Queen's apartments and all. The Queen is very fond of politics."

He was such an amusing vagabond, with his jolly ways and boundless impudence, and so young, that no very serious punishment was then meted out to him, nor even on his second "intrusion," as it was mildly denominated, when he was found crouched in a recess, dragged forth, and taken to the police-station. This time he said he had hidden under a sofa in one of the Queen's private apartments, and had listened to a long conversation between her and Prince Albert. He was sent to the House of Correction for a few months, in the hope of curing him of his "Palace- breaking mania"; but immediately on his liberation, he was found prowling about the Palace, drawing nearer and nearer, as though it had been built of loadstone. But finally he was induced to go to Australia, where, it is said, he grew up to be a well-to-do colonist. Perhaps he met the house- painter Oxford there, and they used to talk over their exploits and explorations together, after the manner of heroes and adventurers, from the time of Ulysses and Æneas. We can imagine the *man* Jones being a particularly entertaining boon companion, with his reminiscences of high life, not only below, but above stairs, in Buckingham Palace. That he ever made an entrance into those august precincts, and was so long undiscovered, certainly speaks not well for the police and domestic arrangements of the household; and it is little wonder that Baron Stockmar was finally sent for to suggest some plan for the better regulation of matters in both the great royal residences. And he did work wonders,—though mostly by inspiring others, the proper officers, to work. This extraordinary man seemed to have a genius for order, discipline, economy, and dispatch. He found the palaces grand "circumlocution offices,"—with, in all the departments, an entangling network of red-tape, which needed to be swept away like cobwebs. He himself entered the Royal Nursery finally with the besom of reform. It is said in his "Memoirs"—"The organization and superintendence of the children's department occupied a considerable portion of Stockmar's time"; and he wrote, "The Nursery gives me more trouble than the government of a King would do." Very likely the English nurses and maids questioned among themselves the right of an old German doctor to meddle with their affairs, and dictate what an English Princess Royal should eat, drink, and wear; but they lived to see the Baron's care and skill make of a delicate child—"a pretty, pale, erect little creature," as she is described, a ruddy and robust little girl, of whom the Baron wrote: "She is as round as a little barrel"; of whom the mother wrote: "Pussy's cheeks are on the point of bursting, they have grown so red and plump."

After the domestic reforms in the Palace, no such adventure could have happened to a guest as that recorded by M. Guizot, who having been unable to summon a servant to conduct him to his room at night, wandered about the halls like poor Mr. Pickwick at the inn, and actually blundered into Her Majesty's own dressing-room. The boy Jones, too, had had his day.

At the very time of the "intrusions" into Buckingham Palace, there was in London another young man, with a "mania for Palace-breaking," of a somewhat different sort. He, too, was "without visible means of support," but nobody called him a vagabond, or a burglar, but only an adventurer, or a "pretender." He had his eye particularly on Royal Windsor, and once a cruel hoax was played off upon him, in the shape of a forged invitation to one of the Queen's grand entertainments at the Castle. He got himself up in Court costume, with the aid of a friend, and went, to be told by the royal porter that his name was not down on the list, and afterwards by a higher officer of the household that really there must be some mistake, for Her Majesty had not the honor of knowing him, so could not receive him. We shall see how it was when he came again, nine or ten years later.

But after all, the French royal palaces were more to this young man's taste, for he was French. He longed to break into the Tuileries—not to hide behind, or under any furniture, but to sit on the grandest piece of furniture there. He had a strange longing for St. Cloud, and Fontainebleau, and even stately Versailles. Said of him one English statesman to another, "Did you ever know such a fool as that fellow is? Why, he really believes he will yet be Emperor of France."

That "fellow" was Louis Napoleon Bonaparte.

In August of this year, the Whig Ministry finding themselves a minority in the new Parliament, resigned, and a Conservative one was formed, with Sir Robert Peel as Premier. It came hard for the Queen to part with her favorite Minister and faithful friend, Lord Melbourne, but she soon became reconciled to his Tory successor, and things went on very harmoniously. The benign influence and prudent counsels of Prince Albert, with some lessons of experience, and much study of her constitutional restrictions, as well as obligations, had greatly modified Her Majesty's strong partisan prejudices, and any proclivities she may have had toward personal and irresponsible government.

One great thing in favor of the new Minister, was that he thoroughly appreciated Prince Albert. One of his early acts was to propose a Fine Arts Commission—having for its chief, immediate object, the superintendence of the artistic work on the new Houses of Parliament. This was formed—composed of some of the most eminent artists and *connaisseurs* in the kingdom, and Prince Albert was the chairman. He used to speak of this as his "initiation into public life." The Queen rejoiced in it, as in every stage of her husband's advance—which it is only just to say was the advance of the liberal arts in England, as well as of social and political reforms. I believe it is not generally known that to the humane influence of the Prince-Consort with the Duke of Wellington, was owing the new military regulation which finally put an end to duelling in the English army. Lord, keep his memory green!

The second year of the Queen's marriage wore on to November, and again the Archbishops and Bishops, the statesmen and "Medicine men," the good mother-in-law, and the nurses were summoned by the anxious Prince to Buckingham Palace. This time it was a boy, and the holy men and wise men felt that they had not come out so early in the morning and waited four hours in an ante-room for nothing. Prince Albert was overjoyed. Everybody at the Palace was wild with delight, so wild that there was great confusion. Messengers were dispatched right and left to royal relatives. It is said that no less than three arrived within as many minutes, at Marlborough House, to acquaint the Queen Dowager of the happy event. As they came in breathless, one after another, Her Majesty might have supposed that Victoria and Albert had been blessed with triplets. The biggest guns boomed the glad tidings over London,—the Privy Council assembled to consider a form of prayer and thanksgiving, to relieve the overcharged hearts of the people; the bells in all the churches rang joyous peals. So was little Albert Edward ushered into the kingdom he is to rule in God's own time.

No such ado was made over the seven brothers and sisters who came after; but they were made welcome and comfortable, as, alas! few children can be made, even by loving hearts and willing hands. The Queen may have thought of this, and of what a sorry chance some poor little human creatures have, from the beginning, for she did a beautiful thing on this occasion. She notified the Home Secretary that all those convicts who had behaved well, should have their punishment commuted, and that those deserving clemency, on the horrible prison-hulks, should have their liberty at once. She had a right to be happy, and that she was happy, a beautiful picture in her journal shows:

"Albert brought in dearest little Pussy, in such a smart, white morino dress, trimmed with blue, which mama had given her, and a pretty cap, and placed her on my bed, seating himself next to her, and she was very dear and good, and as my precious invaluable Albert sat there, and our little love between us, I felt quite moved with happiness and gratitude to God.".

The next month she wrote from Windsor Castle to her Uncle Leopold: "I wonder very much whom our little boy will be like. You will understand how fervent are my prayers, and I am sure everybody's must be, to see him resemble his father, in every respect, both in mind and body." Later still she writes: "We all have our trials and vexations—but if *one's home is happy*, then the rest is comparatively nothing."

They had an unusually merry Christmas-time at Windsor, and they danced into the new year, in the old English style—only varying it by a very poetic and impressive German custom. As the clock struck twelve, a flourish of trumpets was blown.

The Prince of Wales was christened in the Royal Chapel, at Windsor, with the greatest state and splendor, King Frederick William of Prussia, who had come over for the purpose, standing as chief sponsor. Then followed all sorts of grand festivities and parades—both at Windsor and in London. The Queen did honor to her "brother of Prussia" in every possible way—in banquets and balls, in proroguing Parliament, in

54

holding a Chapter of the Garter, and investing him with the splendid insignia of the Order, and in having a grand inspection for him, of "Prince Albert's Own Hussars," he being a little in the military line himself.

Among the suite of the Prussian King was Baron Alexander Von Humboldt. The great *savant* was treated by the Queen and the Prince with distinguished consideration, then and ever after. The Prince, on hearing of his death in 1859, wrote to the Crown Princess: "What a loss is the excellent Humboldt! You and Berlin will miss him greatly. People of this kind do not grow on every bush, and they are the glory and the grace of a country and a century." When the Baron's private correspondence was published, and found to contain certain slurs and sarcasms regarding him, and, as he affirmed, misrepresentations—probably based on misunderstandings of his political opinions—the Prince showed no resentment, though he must have been wounded. I know nothing more sensible and charitable in all his admirable private writings, than his few words on this unpleasant incident. He says: "The matter is really of no consequence, for what does not one write or say to his intimate friends, under the impulse of the moment. But the publication is a great indiscretion. How many deadly enemies may be made if publicity be given to what one man has said of another, or perhaps has *not* said!"

But what does it matter to the dead, how many "deadly enemies" are made? They have us at unfair advantage. We may deny, we may cry out, but we cannot make them apologize, or retract, or modify the cruel sarcasm, or more cruel ridicule. They seem to stealthily open the door of the tomb, to shoot Parthian arrows at the very mourners who have just piled wreaths before it. Carlyle fired a perfect *mitrailleuse* from his grave. The Prince's English biographer calls the Humboldt publication "scandalous." Yet the English, who sternly condemn the most kindly personalities of living authors (especially American authors), seem to have rather a relish for these peppery posthumous revelations of genius, —often saddening post-mortem exhibitions of its own moral weaknesses and disease. No great English author dies nowadays, without his most attached, faithful and familiar friends being in mortal terror lest they be found spitted on the sharp shafts of his, or worse, *her* satire.

During those Windsor festivities, the little Prince of Wales was shown to the people at an upper window and pronounced satisfactory. A Court lady described him at the time, as "the most magnificent baby in the Kingdom." And perhaps he was. He was fair and plump, with pleasant blue eyes. It seems to me that after all the years, he must look to-day, with his fresh, open face, a good deal as he did on the day when his nurse dandled him at the Castle window. He still has the fairness, the plumpness, the pleasant blue eyes. It is true he has not very abundant hair now, but he had not much then.

Tytler, the historian, gives a charming picture of him. as he appeared some two years later. He was waiting one morning in the corridor at Windsor with others to see the Queen, who came in bowing most graciously, and having by the hand the Prince of Wales, "trotting on, looking happy and merry." When she came to where Mr. Tytler stood, and saw him "bowing and looking delightedly" at the little Prince and her, she bowed and said to the little boy, "Make a bow, sir!" "When the Queen said this, the Duke of Cambridge and the rest stood still, and the little Prince, walking straight up to me, made a bow, smiling all the while, and holding out his hand, which I immediately took, and bowing low, kissed it." The Queen, he added, "smiled affectionately on the little Prince, for the gracious way in which he deported himself."

CHAPTER XVIII.

Miscreants and Monarchs—A visit from Mendelssohn—The Queen's first visit to Scotland—Anecdote—A trip to France and Belgium—Death of the Duke of Sussex and of Prince Albert's father—The Dwarf and the Giant.

This year of 1842 was not all joy and festivity. It was the year of the massacres of the British forces in Cabul; there was financial distress in England, which a charitable masked ball at Buckingham Palace did not wholly relieve; and in May occurred the second attempt on the life of the Queen—that of John Francis.

The Queen behaved with her own wonderful courage on this occasion—which was expected by her and Prince Albert, from their having a strong impression that the same wretch had the day before pointed at them, from the midst of a crowd, a pistol which had missed fire. They drove out alone together, keeping a pretty sharp lookout for the assassin—and at last, they saw him just as he fired. The ball passed under the carriage, and Francis was at once arrested. Lady Bloomfield, who was then Maid of Honor, gives an account of the excitement at the Palace that evening, and quotes some words of the Queen, very beautiful because revealing her rare consideration for others. She says that Sir Robert Peel was there, and showed intense feeling about the risk Her Majesty had run, and that the Queen, turning to her, said: "I dare say, Georgy, you were surprised at not driving with me to-day—but the fact was, that as we were returning from church yesterday, a man presented a pistol at the carriage window. It flashed in the pan, and we were so taken by surprise that he had time to escape. I knew what was hanging over me to-day, and was determined not to expose any life but my own."

Francis was tried and sentenced to death, but through the Queen's clemency the sentence was commuted to transportation for life, and the very day after, Bean, the hunchback, essayed to shoot Her Majesty with a charge of paper and bits of clay-pipe. He was such a miserable, feeble- minded creature, that they only gave him eighteen months' imprisonment.

Soon after, the Queen was called to mourn with her aunt of Belgium, and the rest of the family of Louis Philippe of France, for the death of the Duke of Orleans, who was killed by being thrown from his carriage. If he had lived, Louis Napoleon would hardly have been Emperor of France.

So it was hardly a gay summer for the Queen, though she had some pleasure, especially in receiving Prince Albert's brother, Ernest, Duke of Saxe-Coburg, and his bride, who came to England for their honeymoon. They had also a pleasant visit from the great composer, Mendelssohn, who thus wrote from Windsor to his mother, "Add to this the pretty and most charming Queen Victoria, who looks so youthful, and is so gently courteous and gracious, who speaks such good German, and knows all my music so well,"—great praise from a Teutonic and Mendelssohnian point of view. In the autumn, the Queen and Prince made their first visit to Scotland—were received with immense enthusiasm everywhere, and had a charming and health-bracing tour. They took Edinburgh by surprise— entering the city from the sea, so early in the morning, that the authorities, who had made great preparations to receive them, and rain flowers and speeches upon them, were still in bed. Still the Queen made up for it, by afterwards making a grand State-procession through the grand old town. All the country for many miles about, poured into the city on that day, and among some amusing anecdotes of the occasion, I find this: "A gentleman living near Edinburgh, said to his farm-servant, 'Well, John, did you see the Queen?' 'Troth did I that, sir.' 'Well, what did you think of her?' 'In truth, sir, I was terrible 'feared afore she came forrit—my heart was maist in my mouth, but whan she did come forrit, I was na feared at a'; I just lookit at her, and she lookit at me, an' she bowed her heid at me, an' I bowed my heid at her.'"

The Queen traveled then with a much larger Court than she takes with her nowadays, and to this were added the escorts of honor which the great Scottish nobles and Highland chiefs furnished her, till it grew to be a monster of a caravan. Among the items, I find that in conveying Her Majesty and suite from Dalkeith to Taymouth, and from Taymouth back to Dalkeith, 656 horses were employed. Yet this was nothing to the number of animals engaged on the royal progresses of former times. It is stated that 20,000 horses were in all employed in conveying Marie Antoinette, her enormous suite and cumbrous belongings, from Vienna to Paris. Poor woman!—it took all those horses to bring her into her kingdom, but only one to carry her out of her kingdom, *via* the Place de la Revolution.

In the spring of the year following this tour, another Princess was born in Buckingham Palace, and christened Alice Maud Mary. The summer went by as usual, or even more pleasantly, for every new baby seemed to make this family happier and gayer.

Lady Bloomfield gives some charming pictures of the happy home-life at Windsor—of the children, pretty, merry, healthy, and well-bred; tells very pleasant things of the Queen, and of the sweet and noble Duchess of Kent—but gives only now and then, a glimpse of that gracious and graceful presence, Prince Albert. Her Majesty made the life of her maids of honor almost too easy. No long, tiresome waiting on their poor, tired feet—no long hours of reading aloud, such as poor Miss Burney had to endure, in the time of old Queen Charlotte. Lady Bloomfield—then Georgiana Ravensworth—had little to do but to hand the Queen her bouquet at dinner—to ride out with her and sing with her.

In the summer of 1843, the Queen and Prince made their first visit to the King and Queen of France, at the Chateau d'Eu, near Treport, on the coast. The King and several of his sons came off in the royal barge to meet their yacht, which they boarded. One account says that Louis Philippe, most unceremonious of monarchs, caught up the little Queen, kissed her on both cheeks, and carried her bodily on to his barge.

Two Queens—Marie Amélie of France and her daughter, Louise of Belgium, and two of her daughters-in-law—were at the landing to receive the first Sovereign of England who had ever come to their shores on a friendly, neighborly visit. It was a visit "of unmixed pleasure," says the Queen, and the account of it is very pleasant reading now; but I have not space to reproduce it. One little passage, in reference to the widowed Duchesse d'Orleans, strikes my eye at this moment: "At ten, dear Hélène came to me with little Paris, and stayed till the King and Queen came to fetch us to breakfast."

"Little Paris" is the present Bourbon-Orleanist bugbear of the French Republic—a very tame and well-behaved *bête noir*, but distrusted and dreaded all the same.

After this French visit, the Queen and Prince went over to see their uncle and aunt, at Brussels, and had a very interesting tour through Belgium. Prince Albert, writing to the Baron soon after, said: "We found uncle and aunt well. ... The children are blooming. Little Charlotte is quite the prettiest child you ever saw." This "little Charlotte" afterwards married Maximilian of Austria, the imperial puppet of Louis Napoleon in Mexico. So Charlotte was for a brief, stormy time an Empress —then came misfortune and madness. She is living yet, in that world of shadows so much sadder than "the valley of the shadow of death."

In the spring of this year, the Duke of Sussex died, and at the next prorogation of Parliament I read that the Queen, no longer fearing to wound the susceptibilities of her proud old uncle, said to her husband, "Come up higher!"—and had a chair for him, precisely like her own, on a level with her own. It was on her left. The smaller chair, on her right, belonged to "little Bertie," who was not yet quite ready to occupy it.

In the autumn, came a visit to the University of Cambridge, where the Queen had the delight of seeing the degree of LL.D. conferred on her husband. So he mounted, step by step, into the honorable position which belonged to him. In this year also, he won laurels which he cared little for, but which counted much for him among a class of Englishmen who lightly esteemed his literary, artistic, and scientific taste and knowledge. In a great hunting-party he carried off the honors by his fearless and admirable riding. Sporting men said: "Why, there really is something in the man beside good looks and German music and metaphysics. He can take hedges and ditches as well as degrees."

I do not think Prince Albert did justice to the English people, when, after his father's death, in the following year, he wrote in the first gush of his grief, to the Baron: "Here we sit together, poor Mama, Victoria and I, and weep, with a great, cold public around us, insensible as stone."

I cannot believe that the British public is ever insensible to royal sorrow.

The Prince-Consort went over to Coburg on a visit of condolence. Some passages in his letters to the Queen, who took this first separation from him hard, are nice reading for their homely and husbandly spirit. From the yacht, before sailing, he wrote: "I have been here an hour, and regret the lost time which I might have spent with you. Poor child! you will, while I write, be getting ready for luncheon, and you will find a place vacant where I sat yesterday. In your heart, however, I hope my place will not be vacant. I at least, have you on board with me in spirit. I reiterate my entreaty, 'Bear up! and don't give way to low spirits, but try to occupy yourself as much as possible.'" … "I have got toys for the children, and porcelain views for you." … "Oh! how lovely and friendly is this dear old country. How glad I should be to have my little wife beside me, to share my pleasure."

Miss Mitford, speaking of a desire expressed by the Queen, to see that quaint old place, Strawberry Hill and all its curiosities, says: "Nothing can tend more to ensure popularity than that Her Majesty should partake of the national amusements and the natural curiosity of the more cultivated portion of her subjects."

In such directions, certainly, the Queen was never found wanting in those days. In "natural curiosity" she was a veritable daughter of Eve, and granddaughter of George the Third. She was interested not only in the scientific discoveries, new mechanical inventions, and agricultural improvements which so interested her husband, but in odd varieties of animals and human creatures. She accepted with pleasure the gift of a Liliputian horse, supposed to be the smallest in the world—over five years old, and only twenty-seven and a half inches high—brought from Java, by a sea-captain, who used to take the gallant steed under his arm, and run down-stairs with him; and she very graciously received and was immensely entertained with the distinguished young American, who should have been the Alexander of that Bucephalus—General Tom Thumb. This little *lusus naturæ*, under the masterly management of Mr. Barnum, had made a great sensation in London—which, after the Queen had summoned him two or three times to Windsor, grew into a fashionable furor. Mr. Barnum's description of those visits to the royal palaces is very amusing. They were first received in the grand picture-gallery by the Queen, the Duchess of Kent, Prince Albert, and the usual Court ladies and gentlemen. Mr. Barnum writes: "They were standing at the farther end of the room when the doors were thrown open, and the General walked in, looking like a wax-doll gifted with the powers of locomotion. Surprise and pleasure were depicted on the faces of the royal circle, at beholding this remarkable specimen of humanity, so much smaller than they had evidently expected to see him. The General advanced with a firm step, and as he came within hailing distance, made a graceful bow, and said, 'Good- evening, ladies and gentlemen!'

"A burst of laughter followed this salutation. The Queen then took him by the hand, and led him about the gallery, and asked him many questions, the answers to which kept the party in continual merriment. The General informed the Queen, that her picture-gallery was 'first-rate,' and said he should like to see the Prince of Wales. The Queen replied that the Prince had gone to bed, but that he should see him on a future occasion."

The General then gave his songs, dances, and imitations; and after an hour's talk with Prince Albert and the rest, departed as coolly as he had come, but not as leisurely, as the long backing-out process being too tedious, he varied it with little runs, which drew from the Queen, Prince, and Court peels of laughter, and roused the ire of the Queen's poodle, who attacked the small Yankee stranger. The General defended himself with his little cane, as valiantly as the original Tom Thumb with his mother's darning-needle. On the next visit, he was introduced to the Prince of Wales, whom he addressed with a startling, "How are you, Prince?" He then received a costly souvenir from the Queen, and, each time he performed, generous pay in gold. The Queen Dowager was also much taken with him, and presented him with a beautiful little watch. She called him "dear little General," and took him on her lap. The time came (when this "full-grown" dwarf was fuller-grown) that the most powerful Queen Dowager would have found it difficult to dandle him, Charles Stratton, Esq., a husband and father, on her knee: The fact is the General was a bit of a humbug, being considerably younger than he was given out to be. But he was an exceedingly pretty, amusing little humbug, so it was no matter then. But when the truth came out, the Queen's faith in Yankee showmen must have suffered a shock, as must that of the honest old Duke of Wellington, who used to drop in at Egyptian Hall so often to see the tiny creature assume the dress and the pensive pose of Napoleon "thinking of the loss of the battle of Waterloo," and looking so like his old enemy, seen through a reversed field-glass. Very likely the Queen's "full-grown" Java horse turned out to be a young colt.

After the dwarf, came the giant—the tallest and grandest of the sovereigns of Europe, Nicholas, the Emperor of all the Russias. He came on one of his war-ships, but with the friendliest feelings, and "just dropped in" on the Queen, with only a few hours' notice. It was a pleasant little way he had of surprising his friends. However, he was made welcome, and everything possible was done to entertain and do him honor during his stay. He had visited England before, when he was much younger and handsomer. Baron Stockmar met him at Claremont, in the time of the Princess Charlotte and Prince Leopold, and quotes a compliment paid him by a Court lady, in the refined language of the Regency: "What an amiable creature! He is devilish handsome! He will be the handsomest man in Europe." And so he might have been, had he possessed a heart and soul. But his expression was always, if not actually bad, severe and repellant. The look his large, keen eyes, which had very pale lashes, and every now and then showed the white all round the iris, is said to have been quite awful. He was a soldier above all things, and told the Queen he felt very awkward in evening-dress, as though in leaving off his uniform he had "taken off his skin." He must have been rather a discommoding guest, from a little whim he had of sleeping only on straw. He always had with him a leathern case, which at every place he stopped, was filled with fresh straw from the stables.

He was an excessively polite man—this towering Czar; but for all that, a very cruel man—a colossal embodiment of the autocratic principle— selfish and cold and hard—though he did win upon the Queen's heart by praise of her husband. He said: "Nowhere will you find a handsomer young man; he has such an air of nobility and goodness." It was a mystery how he could so well appreciate that pure and lovable character, for the Prince Consort must always have been a mystery to men like the Czar Nicholas.

CHAPTER XIX.

Old homes and new—A visit from the King of France—The Queen and Prince Albert make their first visit to Germany—Incidents of the trip—A new seaside home on the Isle of Wight—Repeal of the Corn Laws—Prince Albert elected Chancellor of Cambridge University—Benjamin Disraeli.

This year—1844—there was a death in the household at Windsor, and a birth. The death was that of Eos, the favorite greyhound of Prince Albert. "Dear Eos," as the Queen called her, was found dead one morning. The Prince wrote the next day to his grandmother, "You will share my sorrow at this loss. She was a singularly clever creature and had been for eleven years faithfully devoted to me. How many recollections are linked with her."

This beautiful and graceful animal, almost human in her love, and in something very like intellect and soul, appears in several of Landseer's pictures. I will not apologize for keeping a Royal Prince waiting while I give this space to her. This Prince, born at Windsor, in August, was the present Duke of Edinburgh. He was christened Alfred Ernest Albert. The Queen in her journal wrote: "The scene in the chapel was very solemn. ... To see those two children there too" (the Princess Royal and the Prince of Wales), "seemed such a dream to me. May God bless them all, poor little things!" Her Majesty adds that all through the service she fervently prayed that this boy might be "as good as his beloved father." How is it, your Royal Highness?

This year they went again to the Highlands for a few weeks. The Queen's journal says: "Mama came to take leave of us. Alice and the baby were brought in, poor little things! to bid us good-bye. Then good Bertie came down to see us, and Vicky appeared as *voyageuse*, and was all impatience to go."

"Bertie" is the family name for the Prince of Wales. I believe that at heart he is still "good Bertie." "Vicky" was the Princess Royal. The Queen further on remarks: "I said to Albert I could hardly believe that our child was traveling with us; it put me so in mind of myself when I was the little Princess.'"

This year Louis Philippe came over to return the visit of the Queen and the Prince, and there were great festivities and investings at Windsor with all possible kindness and courtesy, and I hope the wily old King went home with gratitude in his heart, as well as the garter on his leg. This year too the Queen and Prince made their first visit to Germany together. The picture the Queen paints of the morning of leaving and the parting from the children is very domestic, sweet, and motherly: "Both Vicky and darling Alice were with me while I dressed. Poor dear Puss wished much to go with us and often said, 'Why am I not going to Germany?' Most willingly would I have taken her. I wished much to take one of dearest Albert's children with us to Coburg; but the journey is a serious undertaking and she is very young still." ... "It was a painful moment to drive away with the three poor little things standing at the door. God bless them and protect them—which He will."

The English Queen and the Prince-Consort were received with all possible royal honors and popular respect at Aix-la-Chapelle and Cologne, and at the Royal Palace at Brühl. It was past midnight when they reached that welcome resting-place, and yet, as an account before me states, they were regaled by a military serenade "in which seven hundred performers were engaged!" A German friend of ours from that region supplements this story by stating that five hundred of those military performers were drummers; that they were accompanied by torch-bearers; that they came under the Queen's windows, wakened her out of her first sleep, and almost drove her wild with fright. With those tremendous trumpetings and drum-beatings, "making night hideous" with their storm of menacing, barbaric sound, and with the fierce glare of the torchlight, it might have seemed to her that Doomsday had burst on the world, and that the savage old Huns of Attila were up first, ready for war.

The next day they all went up the Rhine to the King's Palace of Stolzenfels. Never perhaps was even a Rhine steamer so heavily freighted with royalty—a cargo of Kings and Queens, Princes and Archdukes. It was all very fine, as were the royal feasts and festivals, but the Queen and Prince were happiest when they had left all this grandeur and parade behind them and were at Coburg amid their own kin—for there, impatiently awaiting them, were the mother of Victoria and the brother of Albert, and "a staircase full of cousins," as the Queen says. They stopped at lovely Rosenau, and the Queen, with one of her beautiful poetic impulses, chose for their chamber the room in which her husband was born. She wrote in her journal, "How happy, how joyful we were, on awaking, to find ourselves here, at the dear Rosenau, my Albert's birth-place, the place he most loves. … He was so happy to be here with me. It was like a beautiful dream."

The account of the rejoicings of the simple Coburg people, and especially of the children, over their beloved Prince, and over the visit of his august wife, is really very touching. Their offerings and tributes were mostly flowers, poems and music—wonderfully sweet chorales and gay *réveils* and inspiriting marches. There was a great *fête* of the peasants on Prince Albert's birthday, with much waltzing, and shouting, and beer-quaffing, and toast-giving. The whole visit was an Arcadian episode, simple and charming, in the grand royal progress of Victoria's life. But the royal progress had to be resumed—the State called back its bond-servants; and so, after a visit to the dear old grandmother at Gotha—the parting with whom seemed especially hard to Prince Albert, as though he had a presentiment it was to be the last— they set out for home. They took their yacht at Antwerp, and after a flying visit to the King and Queen of France at Eu, were soon at Osborne, where their family were awaiting them. The Queen wrote: "The dearest of welcomes greeted us as we drove up straight to the house, for there, looking like roses, so well and so fat, stood the four children, much pleased to see us!"

Ah, often the best part of going away is coming home.

During this year the Royal Family were very happy in taking possession of their new seaside palace on the Isle of Wight, and I believe paid no more visits to Brighton, which was so much crowded in the season as to make anything like the privacy they desired impossible. During her last stay at the Pavilion the Queen was so much displeased at the rudeness of the people who pressed about her and Prince Albert, when they were trying to have a quiet little walk on the breezy pier, that I read she appealed to the magistrates for protection. There was such a large and ever-growing crowd of excited, hurrying, murmuring, staring Brightonians and strangers about them that it seemed a rallying cry had gone through the town, from lip to lip: "The Queen and Prince are out! To the pier! To the pier!"

The Pavilion was never a desirable Marine Palace, as it commanded no good views of the sea; so Her Majesty's new home in the Isle of Wight had for her, the Prince and the children every advantage over the one in Brighton except in bracing sea-air. Osborne has a broad sea view, a charming beach, to which the woods run down—the lovely woods in which are found the first violets of the spring and to which the nightingales first come. The grounds were fine and extensive, to the great delight of the Prince Consort, who had not only a peculiar passion, but a peculiar talent for gardening. Indeed, when this many-sided German was born a Prince, a masterly landscape-gardener was lost to the world—that is, the world outside the grounds of Windsor, Osborne and Balmoral, which indeed "keep his memory green." The Queen writing from Osborne says: "Albert is so happy here—out all day planting, directing, etc., and it is so good for him. It is a relief to get away from the bitterness which people create for themselves in London."—But I am not writing the Life of Prince Albert;—I often forget that.

The year of 1846 was gloriously marked by the repeal of the Corn Laws; a measure of justice and mercy, the withholding of which from the people had for several years produced much distress and commotion. Some destructive work had been done by mobs on the houses of the supporters of the old laws; they had even stoned the town residence of the Duke of Wellington, Apsley House. The stern old fighter would have been glad at the moment to have swept the streets clear with cannon, but he contented himself with putting shutters over his broken windows, to hide the shame. I believe they were never opened again while he lived. The great leaders in this Corn Laws agitation were Mr. Cobden and Mr. Bright. These great- hearted men could not rest for the cries which came up to them from the suffering people. There were sore privations and "short commons" in

England, and in Ireland, starvation, real, honest, earnest starvation. The poverty of the land had struck down into the great Irish stand-by, the potato, a deadly blight. A year or two later the evil took gigantic proportions; the news came to us in America, and an alarm was sounded which roused the land. We sent a divine Armada against the grim enemy which was wasting the Green Isle; ships, which poured into him broadsides of big bread-balls, and grape-shot of corn, beans and potatoes. It is recorded that "in one Irish seaport town the bells were kept ringing all day in honor of the arrival of one of these grain-laden vessels." I am afraid these bells had a sweeter sound to the poor people than even those rung on royal birthdays.

Strangely enough, after the passage of measures which immortalized his ministerial term, Sir Robert Peel was ejected from power. The Queen parted from him with great regret, but quietly accepted his successor, Lord John Russell.

Six years had now gone by since the marriage of Victoria and Albert, and the family had grown to be six, and soon it was seven, for in May the Princess Helena Augusta Victoria was born. Her godmother was Hélène, the widowed Duchess of Orleans, the mother of the gallant young men, the Count de Paris and the Duke de Chartres, who during our great war came over to America to see service under General McClellan.

About this time the Prince-Consort was called to Liverpool to open a magnificent dock named after him, which duty he performed in the most graceful manner. The next day he laid the foundation-stone for a Sailors' Home. The Queen, who was not able to be with him on these occasions, wrote to the Baron: "I feel very lonely without my dear master, and though I know other people are often separated, I feel that I could never get accustomed to it. … Without him everything loses its interest. It will always cause a terrible pang for me to be separated from him even for two days, and I pray God not to let me survive him. I glory in his being seen and loved."

In September they went into the new Marine Palace at Osborne. On the first evening, amid the gaieties of the splendid house-warming festival, the Prince very solemnly repeated a hymn of Luther's, sung in Germany on these occasions. Translated it is:

"God bless our going out, nor less
Our coming in, and make them sure;
God bless our daily bread, and bless
Whate'er we do—whate'er endure;
In death unto His peace awake us,
And heirs of His salvation make us."

They were very happy amid all the political trouble and perplexity— almost too happy, considering how life was going on, or going off in poor Ireland. Doubtless the cries of starving children and the moans of fever- stricken mothers must often have pierced the tender hearts of the Queen and Prince; but the calamity was so vast, so apparently irremediable, that they turned their thoughts away from it as much as possible, as we turn ours from the awful tragic work of volcanoes in the far East and tornadoes in the West. It was a sort of charmed life they lived, with its pastoral peace and simple pleasures. Lady Bloomfield wrote: "It always entertains me to see the little things which amuse Her Majesty and the Prince, instead of their looking bored, as people so often do in English society." One thing, however, did "bore" him, and that, unfortunately, was riding—"for its own sake." So it was not surprising that after a time the Queen indulged less in her favourite pastime. She still loved a romping dance now and then, but she was hardly as gay as when Guizot first saw and described her. Writing from Windsor to his son he gives a picture of a royal dinner party: "On my left sat the young Queen whom they tried to assassinate the other day, in gay spirits, talking a great deal, laughing very often and longing to laugh still more; and filling with her gaiety, which contrasted with the already tragical elements of her history, this ancient castle which has witnessed the career of all her predecessors."

The political affairs which tried and troubled the Queen and the Prince were not merely English. They were much disturbed and shocked by the unworthy intrigues and the unkingly bad faith shown by Louis Philippe in the affair of the "Spanish Marriages"—a complicated and rather delicate matter, which I have neither space nor desire to dwell upon here. It had a disastrous effect on the Orleans family, and perhaps on the history of France. It has been mostly interesting to me now for the manner in which the subject was handled by the Queen, whose letters revealed a royal high spirit and a keen sense of royal honor. She regretted the heartless State marriage of the young Queen of Spain, not only from a political but a domestic point of view. She saw poor Isabella forced or tricked into a distasteful union, from which unhappiness must, and something far worse than unhappiness might, come. Many and great misfortunes did come of it and to the actors in it.

In the spring of 1847 the Prince-Consort was elected Chancellor of the University of Cambridge—a great honor for so young a man. The Queen was present at the installation, and there was a splendid time. Wordsworth wrote an ode on the occasion. It was not quite equal to his "Ode on the Intimations of Immortality." In truth, Mr. Wordsworth did not shine as Poet Laureate. Mr. Tennyson better earns his butt of Malmsey.

Seated on the throne in the great Hall of Trinity, the Queen received the new Chancellor, who was beautifully dressed in robes of black and gold, with a long train borne by two of his officers. He read to her a speech, to which she read a reply, saying that on the whole she approved of the choice of the University. "I cannot say," writes the Queen, "how it agitated and embarrassed me to have, to receive this address, and hear it read by my beloved Albert, who walked in at the head of the University, and who looked dear and beautiful in his robes."

Happy woman! When ordinary husbands make long, grave speeches to their wives, they do not often look "dear and beautiful!"

This year a new prima-donna took London by storm and gave the Queen and Prince "exquisite enjoyment." Her Majesty wrote: "Her acting alone is worth going to see, and the *piano* way she has of singing, Lablache says, is unlike anything he ever heard. He is quite enchanted. There is a purity in her singing and acting which is quite indescribable."

That singer was Jenny Lind.

About this time lovers of impassioned oratory felt the joy which the astronomer knows "*when a new comet swims into his ken*" in the appearance of a brilliant political orator, of masterly talent and more masterly will. This still young man of Hebraic origin, rather dashing and flashing in manner and dress, had not been thought to have any very serious purpose in life, and does not seem to have much impressed the Queen or Prince Albert at first; but the time came when he, as a Minister and friend, occupied a place in Her Majesty's respect and regard scarcely second to the one once occupied by Lord Melbourne. This orator was Benjamin Disraeli.

CHAPTER XX.

A Troublous Time—Louis Philippe an Exile—The Purchase of Balmoral—A Letter of Prince Albert's—Another attempt on the Queen's Life—The Queen's instructions to the Governess of her Daughters—A visit to Ireland—Death of Dowager Queen Adelaide.

At last came 1848—a year packed with political convulsions and overthrows. The spirit of revolution was rampant, bowling away at all the thrones of Europe. England heard the storm thundering nearly all round the horizon, for in the sister isle the intermittent rebellion broke out, chiefly among the "Young Ireland" party, led by Mitchel, Meagher and O'Brien. This plucky little uprising was soon put down. The leaders were brave, eloquent, ardent young men, but their followers were not disposed to fight long and well—perhaps their stomachs were too empty. The Chartists stirred again, and renewed their not unreasonable or treasonable demands; but all in vain. There is really something awful about the strength and solidity and impassivity of England. When the French monarchy went down in the earthquake shock of that wild winter, and a republic came up in its place, it surely would have been no wonder if a vast tidal-wave of revolution caused by so much subsidence and upheaving had broken disastrously on the English shores. But it did not. The old sea-wall of loyalty and constitutional liberty was too strong. There were only floated up a few waifs, and among them a "*forlorn and shipwrecked brother*," calling himself "John Smith," and a poor, gray- haired, heart-broken woman, "Mrs. Smith," for the nonce. When these came to land they were recognized as Louis Philippe and Marie Amélie of France. Afterwards most of their family, who had been scattered by the tempest, came also, and joined them in a long exile. The English asylum of the King and Queen was Claremont, that sanctuary of love and sorrow, which the Queen, though loving it well, had at once given over to her unfortunate old friends, whom she received with the most sympathetic kindness, trying to forget all causes of ill-feeling given her a year or two before by the scheming King and his ambitious sons.

In the midst of the excitement and anxiety of that time, a gentle, loving, world-wearied soul passed out of our little mortal day at Gotha, and a fresh, bright young soul came into it in London. The dear old grandmother of the Prince died, in her palace of Friedrichsthal, and his daughter, Louise Caroline Alberta, now Marchioness of Lorne, was born in Buckingham Palace.

Among those ruined by the convulsions in Germany were the Queen's brother, Prince Leiningen, and her brother-in-law, Prince Hohenlohe. So the thunderbolt had struck near. At one time it threatened to strike still nearer, for that spring the Chartists made their great demonstration, or rather announced one. It was expected that they would assemble at a given point and march, several hundred thousand strong, on Parliament, bearing a monster petition. What such a mighty body of men might do, what excesses they might commit in the capital, nobody could tell. The Queen was packed off to Osborne with baby Louise, to be out of harm's way, and 170,000 men enrolled themselves as special constables. Among these was Louis Napoleon, longing for a fight of some sort in alliance with England. He did net get it till some years after. There was no collision, in fact no large compact procession; the Chartists, mostly very good citizens, quietly dispersed and went home after presenting their petition. The great scare was over, but the special constables were as proud as Wellington's army after Waterloo.

When the Chartist leaders had been tried for sedition and sentenced to terms of imprisonment, and the Irish leaders had been transported, things looked so flat in England that the young French Prince turned again to France to try his fortune. It was his third trial. The first two efforts under Louis Philippe to stir up a revolt and topple the citizen king from the throne had ended in imprisonment and ridicule; but now he would not seem to play a Napoleonic game. He would fall in with republican ideas and run for the Presidency, which he did, and won. But as the countryman at the circus, after creating much merriment by his awkward riding in his rural costume, sometimes throws it off and appears as a spangled hero and the very prince of equestrians; so this "nephew of his uncle," suddenly emerging from the disguise of a republican President, blazed forth a full-panoplied warrior-Emperor. But this was not yet.

In September of this year the Queen and Prince first visited a new property they had purchased in the heart of the Highlands. The Prince wrote of it: "We have withdrawn for a short time into a complete mountain solitude, where one rarely sees a human face, where the snow already covers the mountain-tops and the wild deer come creeping stealthily round the house. I, naughty man, have also been creeping stealthily after the harmless stags, and today I shot two red deer." ... "The castle is of granite, with numerous small turrets, and is situated on a rising-ground, surrounded by birchwood, and close to the river Dee. The air is glorious and dear, but icy cold."

What a relief it must have been to them to feel themselves out of the reach of runaway royalties, and "surprise parties" of Emperors and Grand Dukes.

In March, 1849, the Prince laid the foundation-stone for the Great Grimsby Docks, and made a noble speech on the occasion. From that I will not quote, but I am tempted to give entire a charming note which he wrote from Brocklesby, Lord Yarborough's place, to the Queen.

It runs thus:

"Your faithful husband, agreeably to your wishes, reports: 1. That he is still alive. 2. That he has discovered the North Pole from Lincoln Cathedral, but without finding either Captain Ross or Sir John Franklin. 3. That he arrived at Brocklesby and received the address. 4. That he subsequently rode out and got home quite covered with snow and with icicles on his nose. 5. That the messenger is waiting to carry off this letter, which you will have in Windsor by the morning. 6. Last, but not least, that he loves his wife and remains her devoted husband."

We may believe the good, fun-loving wife was delighted with this little letter, and read it to a few of her choicest friends.

A few months later, while the Queen was driving with her children in an open carriage over that assassin-haunted Constitution Hill, she was fired at by a mad Irishman— William Hamilton. She did not lose for a moment her wonderful self-possession, but ordered the carriage to move on, and quieted with a few calm words the terror of the children.

We have seen that at the time of Oxford's attempt she "laughed at the thing"; but now there had been so many shootings that "the thing" was getting tiresome and monotonous, and she did not interfere with the carrying out of the sentence of seven years' transportation. This was not the last. In 1872 a Fenian tried his hand against his widowed sovereign, and we all know of the shocking attempt of two years ago at Windsor. In truth, Her Majesty has been the greatest royal target in Europe. *Messieurs les assassins* are not very gallant.

All this time the Prince-Consort was up to his elbows in work of many kinds. That which he loved best, planning and planting the grounds of Osborne and Balmoral and superintending building, he cheerfully sacrificed for works of public utility. He inaugurated and urged forward many benevolent and scientific enterprises, and schools of art and music. This extraordinary man seemed to have a prophetic sense of the value and ultimate success of inchoate public improvements, and when he once adopted a scheme allowed nothing to discourage him. He engineered the Holborn Viaduct enterprise, and I notice that at a late meeting of the brave Channel Tunnel Company, Sir E. W. Watkin claimed that "the cause had once the advocacy of the great Prince-Consort, the most sagacious man of the century."

With all these things he found time to carefully overlook the education of his children. The Prince of Wales was now thought old enough to be placed under a tutor, and one was selected—a Mr. Birch (let us hope the name was not significant), "a young, good-looking, amiable man," who had himself taken "the highest honors at Cambridge";— doubtless a great point those highest Cambridge honors, for the instructor of an eight-years-old boy. For all the ability and learning of his tutor, it is said that the Prince of Wales never took to the classics with desperate avidity. He was never inclined to waste his strength or dim his pleasant blue eyes over the midnight oil.

65

Prince Albert never gave the training of his boys up wholly to the most accomplished instructors. His was still, while he lived, the guiding, guarding spirit. The Queen was equally faithful in the discharge of her duties to her children—especially to her daughters. In her memoranda I find many admirable passages which reveal her peculiarly simple, domestic, affectionate system of home government. The religious training of her little ones she kept as much as possible in her own hands, still the cares of State and the duties of royal hospitality would interfere, and, writing of the Princess Royal, in 1844, she says: "It is a hard case for me that my occupations prevent me from being with her when she says her prayers."

Some instructions which she gave to this child's governess should be printed in letters of gold:

"I am quite clear that she should be taught to have great reverence for God and for religion, but that she should have the feeling of devotion and love which our heavenly Father encourages His earthly children to have for Him, and not one of fear and trembling; and that thoughts of death and an after life should not be represented in an alarming and forbidding view; and that she should be made to know as yet no difference of creeds, and not think that she can only pray on her knees, or that those who do not kneel are less fervent or devout in their prayers."

In August of this year the Queen and Prince sailed in their favorite yacht, the *Victoria and Albert*, for Ireland, taking with them their three eldest children, the better to show the Irish people that their sovereign had not lost confidence in them for their recent bit of a rebellion, which she believed was one-half Popery and the other half potato-rot. The Irish people justified that faith. At the Cove of Cork, where the Royal party first landed, and which has been Queenstown ever since, their reception was most enthusiastic, as it was also in Dublin, so lately disaffected. The common people were especially delighted with the children, and one "stout old woman" shouted out, "Oh, Queen, dear, make one o' thim darlints Patrick, and all Ireland will die for ye!" They afterwards got their "Patrick" in the little Duke of Connaught, but I fear were none the more disposed to die for the English Queen. Perhaps he came a little too late.

The Queen on this trip expressed the intention of creating the Prince of Wales Earl of Dublin, by way of compliment and conciliation, and perhaps she did, but still Fenianism grew and flourished In Ireland.

The passage from Belfast to Loch Ryan was very rough—a regular rebellion against, "the Queen of the Seas," as the Emperor of France afterwards called Victoria. She records that, "Poor little Affie was knocked down and sent rolling over the deck, and was completely drenched." The poor little fellow, Prince Alfred, Duke of Edinburgh, the bold mariner of the family, probably cried out then that he would "never, never be a sailor."

In a letter from Balmoral, written on his thirtieth birthday, the Prince- Consort says: "Victoria is happy and cheerful—the children are well and grow apace; the Highlands are glorious."

I do not know that the fact has anything to do with Her Majesty's peculiar love for Scotland, but she came very near being born in that part of her dominions—the Duke of Kent having proposed a little while before her birth to take a place in Lanarkshire, belonging to a friend. Had he done so his little daughter would have been a Highland lassie. I don't think the Queen would have objected. She said to Sir Archibald Alison, "I am more proud of my Scotch descent than of any other. When I first came into Scotland I felt as if I were coming home."

With the occupation of Balmoral this home feeling increased: The Queen was ever impatient to seek that mountain retreat and regretful to leave it. She loved above all the outdoor life there—the rough mountaineering, the deer hunts, the climbing, the following up and fording streams, the picnics on breezy hill-sides; she loved to get out from under the dark purple shadow of royalty and nestle down among the brighter purple of the heather; she loved to go off on wild incognito expeditions and be addressed by the simple peasants without her awesome titles; even loved to be at times like the peasants in simplicity and naturalness, to feel with her "guid mon," like a younger Mistress Anderson with her "jo John." She seemed to enjoy all weathers at Balmoral. I am told that she used to delight in walking in the rain and wind and going out protected only by a thick water-proof, the hood drawn over her head; and that she liked nothing better than driving in a heavy snow-storm. After the return from Scotland, the Queen was to have opened the new Coal Exchange in London, but was prevented by an odd and much-belated ailment, an attack of chicken-pox. Prince Albert went in her place and took the Princess Royal and the Prince of Wales, who, Lady Lyttelton writes: "behaved very civilly and nicely." There was an immense crowd, all shouting and cheering, and smiling kindly on the children. Some official of immense size, with a big cloak and wig, and a big voice, is described as making a pompous speech to little Albert Edward, looking down on him and addressing him as "Your Royal Highness, the pledge, and promise of a long race of Kings." Lady Lyttelton adds: "Poor Princey did not seem to guess at all what he meant."

Soon after this grand affair, a very *grand personage* came not unwillingly to the end of all earthly affairs. Adelaide, Dowager Queen of England, died after a long and painful illness. She had lived a good life; she was a sweet, charitable, patient, lovable woman. The Queen and Prince-Consort were deeply grieved. The Queen wrote: "She was truly motherly in her kindness to us and our children. … Poor mama is very much cut up by this sad event. To her the Queen is a great and serious loss."

Queen Adelaide left directions that her funeral should be as private as possible, and that her coffin should be carried by sailors—a tribute to the memory of the Sailor-King.

From an English gentleman, who has exceptional opportunities of knowing much of the private history of Royalty, I have received an anecdote of this good woman and wife, when Duchess of Clarence—something which our friend thinks does her more honor than afterwards did her title of Queen. When she was married she knew, for everybody knew, of the left-hand marriage of the Duke with the beautiful actress, Mrs. Jordan, from whom he was then separated. The Duke took his bride to Bushey Park, his residence, for the honeymoon, and himself politely conducted her to her chamber. She looked about the elegant room well pleased, but was soon struck by the picture of a very lovely woman, over the mantel. "Who is that?" she asked. The poor Duke was aghast, but he had at least the kingly quality of truth-telling, and stammered out: "That, my dear Adelaide, is a portrait of Mrs. Jordan. I humbly beg your pardon for its being here. I gave orders to have it removed, but those stupid servants have neglected to do it. I will have it done at once— only forgive me."

The Duchess took her husband's hand and said: "No, my dear William, you must not do it! I know what Mrs. Jordan has been to you in the past—that you have loved her—that she is the mother of your children, and I wish her portrait to remain where it is." And it did remain. This was very noble and generous, certainly; but I cannot help thinking that the Duchess was not very much in love.

CHAPTER XXI

The Great Exhibition—Birth of the Duke of Connaught—Death of Sir Robert Peel and Louis Philippe—Prince Albert's speech before the Society for the Propagation of the Gospel in Foreign Parts.

Early in this year of 1850, Prince Albert, though not in his usual health, began in deadly earnest on his colossal labors in behalf of the great "World's Exhibition." England owed that magnificent manifestation of her resources and her enterprise far more to him than to any other man. He met with much opposition from that conservative class who, from the start, denounce all new ideas and innovations, shrinking like owls from the advancing day; and that timid class who, while admitting the grandeur of the idea, feared it was premature. "The time has not come," they said; "wait a century or two." Some opposed it on the ground that it would bring to London a host of foreigners, with foreign ideas and perilous to English morals and religion.

In the garden of a certain grand English country-place there is a certain summer-house with a closed door, which, if a curious visitor opens, lets off some water-works, which give him a spray-douche. So the Prince received, at door after door, a dash of cold water for his "foreign enterprise." But he persevered, letting nothing dishearten him—toiling terribly, and inspiring others to toil, till at last the site he desired for the building was granted him, and the first Crystal Palace—the first palace for the people in England— went slowly up, amid the sun-dropped shades of Hyde Park. Temporary as was that marvelous structure, destined so soon to pass away, like "the baseless fabric of a vision," I can but think it the grandest of the monuments to the memory of the Prince- Consort, though little did he so regard it. To his poetic yet practical mind it was the universal temple of industry and art, the valhalla of the heroes of commerce, the fane of the gods of science—the caravansery of the world. That Exhibition brought together the ends of the earth,—long- estranged human brethren sat down together in pleasant communion. It was a modern Babel, finished and furnished, and where there was almost a fusion, instead of, a confusion, of tongues. The "barbarous Turk" was there, the warlike Russ, the mercenary Swiss, the passionate Italian, the voluptuous Spaniard, the gallant Frenchman,—and yet foreboding English citizens did not find themselves compelled to go armed, or to lock up their plate, or their wives and daughters. In fact, this beautiful realized dream, this accomplished fact, quickened the pulses of commerce, the genius of invention, the soul and the arm of industry, the popular zeal for knowledge, as nothing had ever done before.

To go back a little to family events:—On May 1st, 1850, Prince Albert, in writing to his step-mother at Coburg, told a bit of news very charmingly: "This morning, after rather a restless night (being Walpurgis night, that was very appropriate), and while the witches were careering on the Blocksberg, under Ernst Augustus' mild sceptre, a little boy glided into the light of day and has been received by the sisters with *jubilates*. 'Now we are just as many as the days of the week!' was the cry, and a bit of a struggle arose as to who was to be Sunday. of well-bred courtesy the honor was conceded to the new-comer. Victoria is well, and so is the child."

This Prince was called Arthur William Patrick Albert. The first name was in honor of the Duke of Wellington, on whose eighty-first birthday the boy was born; William was for the Prince of Prussia, now Emperor of Germany; Patrick was for Ireland in general, and the "stout old woman" of Dublin in particular.

This year both the Queen and the country lost a great and valued friend in Sir Robert Peel, who was killed by being thrown from his horse. There was much mourning in England among all sorts of people for this rarely noble, unennobled man. The title of Baronet he had. inherited; it is said he declined a grander title, and he certainly recorded in his will a wish that no one of his sons should accept a title on account of *his* services to the country—which was a great thing for a man to do in England; and after his death, his wife was so proud of bearing his name that she declined a peerage offered to her—which was a greater thing for a woman to do in England.

Not long after, occurred the death of the ex-King of France, at Claremont. McCarthy sums up his character very tersely, thus: "The clever, unwise, grand, mean old man." Louis Philippe's meanness was in his mercenary and plotting spirit, when a rich man and a king—his grand qualities were his courage and cheerfulness, when in poverty and exile.

The Royal Family again visited Edinburgh, and stopped for a while at Holyrood—that quaint old Palace of poor Mary Stuart, whose sad, sweet memory so pervades it, like a personal atmosphere, that it seems she has only gone but for a little walk, or ride, with her four Maries, and will soon come in, laughing and talking French, and looking passing beautiful. Queen Victoria had then a romantic interest in the hapless Queen of Scots. She said to Sir Archibald Alison, "I am glad I am descended from Mary; I have nothing to do with Elizabeth."

From Edinburgh to dear Balmoral, from whence the Prince writes: "We try to strengthen our hearts amid the stillness and solemnity of the mountains."

The Queen's heart especially needed strengthening, for she was dreading a blow which soon fell upon her in the death of her dearest friend, her aunt, the Queen of the Belgians. She mourned deeply and long for this lovely and gifted woman, this "angelic soul," as Baron Stockmar called her.

On April 29, 1851, the Queen paid a private visit to the Exhibition, and wrote: "We remained two hours and a half, and I came back quite beaten, and my head bewildered from the myriads of beautiful and wonderful things which now quite dazzle one's eyes. Such efforts have been made, and our people have shown such taste in their manufactures. All owing to this great Exhibition, and to Albert—all to *him*!"

May 1st, which was the first anniversary of little Arthur's birth, was the great opening-day, when Princes and people took possession of that mighty crystal temple, and the "Festival of Peace" began.

The Queen's description in her diary is an eloquent outpouring of pride and joy, and gratitude. One paragraph ends with these words: "God bless my dearest Albert. God bless my dearest country, which has shown itself so great to-day! One felt so grateful to the great God, who seemed to pervade and bless all."

Her Majesty wrote that the scene in the Park as they drove through—the countless carriages, the vast crowd, the soldiers, the music, the tumultuous, yet happy excitement everywhere, reminded her of her coronation day; but when she entered that great glass house, over which floated in the sunny air the flags of all nations, within which were the representatives of all nations, and when she walked up to her place in the centre, conducted by the wizard who had conjured up for the world that magic structure, and when the two stood there, with a child on either hand, before the motley multitude, cheering in all languages— then, Victoria *felt her name*, and knew she had come to her real coronation, as sovereign, wife, and mother.

Shortly after this great day, Prince Albert distinguished himself by a remarkably fine speech at an immense meeting of the "Society for the Propagation of the Gospel in Foreign Parts." Such shoals of foreigners being then in London, the Society felt that they must be casting in their nets. Lord John Russell wrote to congratulate the Queen, who, next to the heathen, was most interested in the success of this speech. Her reply was very characteristic. After saying that she had been quite "sure that the Prince would say the right thing, from her entire confidence in his tact and judgment," she added, "The Queen at the risk of not appearing sufficiently modest (and yet why should a Woman ever be modest about her husband's merits?) must say that she thinks Lord John will admit now that the Prince is possessed of very extraordinary powers of mind and heart. She feels so proud of being his wife, that she cannot refrain from paying herself a tribute to his noble character."

Ah, English husbands should be loyal beyond measure to the illustrious lady, who has set such a matchless example of wifely faith, pride and devotion. But it will be a pity if in preaching up to their wives her example, they forget the no less admirable example of the Prince-Consort.

CHAPTER XXII

Close of the Great Exhibition-Anecdote—Louis Kossuth—Napoleon III.—The writer's first visit to England—Description of a Prorogation of Parliament.

The great Exhibition was closed about the middle of October, on a dark and rainy day. The last ceremonies were very solemn and impressive. It had not remained long enough for people to be wearied of it. The Queen, the Prince and their children seemed never to tire of visiting it, and the prospect of a sight of them was one of the greatest attractions of the place to other visitors, especially to simple country-folk—though these were sometimes disappointed at not beholding the whole party wearing crowns and trailing royal robes.

I remember a little anecdote of one of Her Majesty's visits to the Crystal Palace. Among the American manufactures were some fine soaps, and among these a small head, done in white Castile, and so exactly like marble that the Queen doubted the soap story, and in her impulsive, investigating way was about to test it with a scratch of her shawl-pin, when the Yankee exhibitor stayed her hand, and drew forth a courteous apology by the loyal remonstrance—"Pardon, your Majesty,—*it is the head of Washington!*"

Soon after the Princes and Kings went home, there arrived in London a man whose heroism and eloquence had thrilled the hearts and filled the thoughts of the world as those of no monarch living had ever done. He was not received with royal honors, though with some generous enthusiasm, by the people. He was looked upon, in high places as that most forlorn being, an unsuccessful adventurer;—so he turned his face, his sad eyes wistful with one last hope, towards the setting sun. Alas, his own political sun had already set!

This man was Louis Kossuth. About the same time another man, without heroism, without eloquence, but with almost superhuman audacity, struck a famous political blow, in Paris, called a *coup d'état*. He exploded a secret mine, which shattered the republic and heaved him up on to an imperial throne. Of course this successful adventurer was Louis Napoleon.

I cannot find that, as the Prince-President of that poor, poetic, impracticable thing, the French Republic, much notice had been taken of him by the English Government;—but "Emperor" was a more respectable title, even worn in this way, snatched in the twinkling of an eye by a political *prestidigitateur*, and it was of greater worth—it had cost blood. So Napoleon III. was recognized by England, and at last by all great powers—royal and republican. Still, for a while, they showed a wary coldness towards the new Emperor; and he was unhappy because all the great European sovereigns hesitated to concede his equality to the extent of addressing him as "*mon frère*" (my brother). He seemed to take this so to heart that, after this solemn declaration that his empire meant peace and not war, the Queen of England put out her friendly little hand and said frankly, "mon frère"; and the King of Prussia and the Emperor of Austria followed her example; but the Czar of Russia, put his iron-gloved hand behind his back and frowned. Louis Napoleon did not forget that ever—but remembered it "excellent well" a few years later, when he was sending off his noble army to the Crimea.

I find two charming domestic bits, in letters of the Queen and Prince, written in May, 1852, from Osborne. After saying that her birthday had passed very happily and peacefully, Her Majesty adds: "I only feel that I never can be half grateful enough for so much love, devotion and happiness. My beloved Albert was, if possible, more than usually kind and good in showering gifts on me. Mama was most kind, too; and the children did everything they could to please me."

It is pleasant to see that the dear mother and grandmother never forgot those family anniversaries, and never was forgotten.

Prince Albert writes, in a letter to the Dowager Duchess of Saxe-Coburg: "The children are well. They grow apace and develop new virtues daily, and also new naughtinesses. The virtues we try to retain, and the naughtinesses we throw away."

This year was a memorable one for the writer of this little book, for it was that of her first visit to England,—of her first sight of London and Charles Dickens, of Westminster Abbey and the Duke of Wellington, Windsor Castle and Queen Victoria.

I had brought a letter, from one of his most esteemed American friends, to the Earl of Carlisle, and from that accomplished and amiable nobleman I received many courtesies,—chief among them a ticket, which he obtained from Her Majesty direct, to one of her reserved seats in the Peeresses' Gallery of the House of Lords, to witness the prorogation of Parliament. I trust I may be pardoned if I quote a portion of my description of that wonderful sight,—written, ah me! so long ago:

… "I found that my seat was one most desirable both for seeing the brilliant assembly and the august ceremony; it was near the throne, yet commanded a view of every part of the splendid chamber.

"The gallery was soon filled with ladies, all in full-dress, jewels, flowers and plumes. Many of the seats of the Peers were also filled by their noble wives and fair daughters, most superbly and sweetly arrayed… Among those conspicuous for elegance and loveliness were the young Duchess of Northumberland and Lady Clementina Villiers, the famous Court beauty.

"Toward one o'clock the Peers began to come in, clad in their robes of State. Taken as a whole they are a noble and refined-looking set of men. But few eyes dwelt on any of these, when there slowly entered, at the left of the throne, a white-haired old man, pale and spare, bowed with years and honors, the hero of many battles in many lands, the conqueror of conquerors,—the Duke! Leaning on the arm of the fair Marchioness of Douro, he stood, or rather tottered, before us, the grandest ruin in England. He presently retired to don his ducal robes and join the royal party at the entrance by the Victoria tower. … The pious bishops, in their sacerdotal robes, made a goodly show before an ungodly world. The judges came in their black gowns and in all the venerable absurdity of their enormous wigs. Mr. Justice Talfourd the poet, a small, modest-looking man, was quite extinguished by his. The foreign Ministers assembled, nation after nation, making, when standing or seated together, a most peculiar and picturesque group. They shone in all colors and dazzled with stars, orders and jewel-bitted swords. …

"Next to me sat the eleven-year-old Princess Gouromma, daughter of the Rajah of Coorg. The day before she had received Christian baptism, the Queen standing as godmother. She is a pretty, bright-looking child, and was literally loaded with jewels. Opposite her sat an Indian Prince—her father, I was told. He was magnificently attired— girded about with a superb India shawl, and above his dusky brow gleamed star-like diamonds, for the least of which many a hard-run Christian would sell his soul. …

"At last, the guns announced the royal procession, and in a few moments the entire house rose silently to receive Her Majesty. The Queen was conducted by Prince Albert, and accompanied by all the great officers of State. The long train, borne by ladies, gentlemen and pages, gave a certain stateliness to the short, plump little person of the fair sovereign, and she bore herself with much dignity and grace. Prince Albert, it is evident, has been eminently handsome, but he is growing a little stout and slightly bald. Yet he is a man of right noble presence. Her Majesty is in fine preservation, and really a pretty and lovable-looking woman. I think I never saw anything sweeter than her smile of recognition, given to some of her friends in the gallery—to the little Indian Princess in especial. There is much in her face of pure womanliness and simple goodness; yet it is by

71

no means wanting in animated intelligence. In short, after seeing her, I can well understand the loving loyalty of her people, and can heartily join in their prayer of 'God Save the Queen!'

"Her Majesty wore a splendid tiara of brilliants, matched by bracelets, necklace and stomacher. Her soft brown hair was dressed very plainly. Her under-dress was of white satin, striped with gold; her robe was, of course, of purple velvet, trimmed with gold and ermine."

"The Queen desired the lords to be seated, and commanded that her 'faithful Commons' should be summoned. When the members of. the lower House had come in, the speaker read a speech, to which, I have recorded, Her Majesty listened, in a cold, quiet manner, sitting perfectly motionless, even to her fingers and eyelids. The Iron Duke standing at her left, bent, and trembled slightly—supporting with evident difficulty the ponderous sword of State. Prince Albert, sitting tall and soldier- like, in his handsome Field-Marshal's uniform, looked nonchalant and serene, but with a certain far-away expression in his eyes. The Earl of Derby held the crown on its gorgeous-cushion gracefully, like an accomplished waiter presenting a tray of ices. On a like occasion, some time ago, I hear the Duke of Argyle had the ill-luck to drop this crown from the cushion, when some of the costly jewels, jarred from their setting, flew about like so many bits of broken glass. But there was no need to cry, 'Pick up the pieces!'

"After the reading of this speech, certain bills were read to Her Majesty, for her assent, which she gave each time with a gracious inclination of the head, shaking sparkles from her diamond tiara in dew- drops of light. At every token of acquiescence a personage whom I took for a herald, bowed low towards the Queen, then performed a similar obeisance towards the Commons—crying *'La Reine le veut!'*"

"Why he should say it in French—why he did not say "The Queen wills it," in her own English, I don't yet know."

I went on: "This ceremony gone through with, the Lord Chancellor, kneeling at the foot of the throne, presented a copy of the Royal speech to the Queen (I had supposed she would bring it in her pocket), which she proceeded to read, in a manner perfectly simple, yet impressive, and in a voice singularly melodious and distinct. Finer reading I never heard anywhere; every syllable was clearly enunciated, and the emphasis fell with unerring precision, though gently, on the right word.

"The Lord Chancellor having formally announced that Parliament stood prorogued until the 20th of August, Her Majesty rose as majestically as could be expected from one more remarkable for rosy plumptitude than regal altitude; Prince Albert took his place at her side; the crown and sword bearers took theirs in front, the train-bearers theirs in the rear, and the royal procession swept slowly forth, the brilliant house broke up and followed, and so the splendid pageant passed away—faded like a piece of fairy enchantment." That's the way they do it,—except that nowadays the Queen does not read her own speech.

CHAPTER XXIII.

Death of the Duke of Wellington—Birth of the Duke of Albany—The Crimean War—Slanders upon Prince Albert—The Prince of Wales takes a place for the first time upon the Throne—Incidents of Domestic Life—Prince Albert visits the Emperor of France—Incidents of the War.

At Balmoral the following autumn, the Queen heard of the death of her most illustrious subject—the Duke of Wellington, and green are those "Leaves" in the journal of her "life in the Highlands," devoted to his memory. She wrote of him as a sovereign seldom writes of a subject,— glowingly, gratefully, tenderly. "One cannot think of this country, without 'the Duke,' our immortal hero"—she said.

There was a glorious state and popular funeral for the grand old man, who was laid away with many honors and many tears in the crypt of St. Paul's Cathedral, where his brother hero, Nelson, was waiting to receive him.

When early in 1853, the news came to Windsor Castle that the French Emperor had selected a bride, not for her wealth, or high birth, or royal connections, but for her beauty, and grace, and because he loved her, Victoria and Albert, as truly lovers as when they entered the old castle gates, as bride and bridegroom, felt more than ever friendly to him, and desirous that he should have a fair field, if no favor, to show what he could do for France. I am afraid they half forgot the *coup d'état*, and the widows, orphans and exiles it had made.

In April, the Queen's fourth son, who was destined to "carry weight" in the shape of names,—Leopold George Duncan Albert—now Duke of Albany, was born in Buckingham Palace.

During this year "the red planet Mars" was in the ascendant. The ugly Eastern Trouble, which finally culminated in the Crimean War, began to loom in the horizon, and England to stir herself ominously with military preparations. Drilling and mustering and mock combats were the order of the day, and the sound of the big drum was heard in the land. They had a grand battle-rehearsal at Chobham, and the Queen and Prince went there on horseback; she wearing a military riding-habit, and accompanied by the Duke of Coburg and her cousin George, King of Hanover.

The weather was genuine "Queen's weather," bright and warm; but Prince Albert, who returned a few days later, to rough it, in a season of regular camp-life, was almost drowned out of his tent by storms. In fact, the warrior bold went home with a bad cold, which ended in an attack of measles. There was enough of this disease to go through the family, Queen and all. Even the guests took it, the Crown Prince of Hanover and the Duke and Duchess of Coburg, who on going home gave it to the Duke of Brabant and the Count of Flanders. I suppose there never was known such a royal run of measles.

This year the Queen and Prince went again to Ireland, to attend the Dublin Industrial Exhibition, and were received with undiminished enthusiasm. It is remarkable that in Ireland the Queen was not once shot at, or struck in the face, or insulted in any way, as in her own capital. All the most chivalric feeling of that mercurial, but generous people, was called out by the sight of her frank and smiling face. She trusted them, and they proved worthy of the trust.

After their return to Balmoral, the Prince wrote: "We should be happy here were it not for that horrible Eastern complication. A European war would be a terrible calamity. It will not do to give up all hope; still, what we have is small."

It daily grew smaller, as the war-clouds thickened and darkened in the political sky. During those troublous times, when some men's hearts were failing them for fear, and some men's were madly panting for the fray, asking nothing better than to see the Lion of England pitted against the Bear of Russia, the Prince was in some quarters most violently and viciously assailed, as a designing, dangerous "influence behind the throne"— treacherous to England, and so to England's Queen. So industriously was this monstrous slander spread abroad, that the story went, and by some simple souls was believed, that "the blameless Prince" had been arrested for high treason, and lodged in the Tower! Some had it that he had gone in through the old Traitors' Grate, and that they were furbishing up the old axe and block for his handsome head! Then the rumor ran that the Queen had also been arrested, and was to be consigned to the grim old fortress, or that she insisted on going with her husband and sharing his dungeon. Thousands of English. people actually assembled about the Tower to see them brought in,—and yet this was not on All-Fools' Day.

73

Poor Baron Stockmar was also suspected of dark political intrigues and practices detrimental to the peace and honor of England. He was, in fact, accused of being a spy and a conspirator—which was absurdity itself. He was, it seems to me, a high-minded, kindly old man, a political philosopher and moralist—rather opinionated always, and at times a little patronizing towards his royal pupils; but if they did not object to this, it was no concern of other people. He certainly had a shrewd, as well as a philosophic mind— was a sagacious "clerk of the weather" in European politics,—and I suppose a better friend man or woman never had than the Prince and the Queen found in this much distrusted old German Baron.

Though Prince Albert wrote at this time about having "a world of torment," he really took matters very patiently and philosophically. In the devotion of his wife, in the affection of his children, in his beloved organ, "the only instrument," he said, "for expressing one's feelings," he found consolation and peace. He wrote,—"Victoria has taken the whole affair greatly to heart, and is excessively indignant at the attacks." But a triumphant refutation, in both Houses of Parliament, of all these slanders, consoled her much; and on the anniversary of her marriage she was able to write—"This blessed day is full of joyful and tender emotions. Fourteen happy years have passed, and I confidently trust many more will pass, and find us in old age, as we are now, happily and devotedly united! Trials we must have; but what are they if we are together?"

In March, 1854, the Queen and Prince went to Osborne to visit the magnificent fleet of vessels which had been assembled at Spithead. Her Majesty wrote to Lord Aberdeen— "We are just starting to see the fleet, which is to sail at once for its important destination. It will be a solemn moment! Many a heart will be very heavy, and many a prayer, including our own, will be offered up for its safety and glory!"

Ah! when those beautiful ships went sailing away, with their white sails spread, and the royal colors flying, death sat "up aloft," instead of the "sweet little cherub" popularly supposed to be perched there, and winds from the long burial-trenches of the battle-field played among the shrouds.

King Frederick William of Prussia seemed to think that he could put an end to this little unpleasantness, and wrote a long letter to the Queen of England, paternally advising her to make some concessions to the Emperor of Russia, which concessions she thought would be weak and unworthy. Her reply reveals her characteristic high courage. One quotation, which she makes from Shakspeare, is admirable:

"Beware
Of entrance to a quarrel; but being in,
Bear't, that the opposed may beware,
of thee."

Still, as we look back, it does seem as though with the wit of the Queen, the wisdom of Prince Albert, the philosophy of Baron Stockmar,—the philanthropy of Exeter Hall, and the piety of the Bench of Bishops, some sort of peaceful arrangement might have been effected, and the Crimean war left out of history. But then we should not have had the touching picture of the lion and the unicorn charging on the enemy together, not for England or France, but all for poor Turkey; and Mr. Tennyson could not have written his "Charge of the Light Brigade," which would have been a great loss to elocutionists. There were in Parliament a few poor- spirited economists and soft-hearted humanitarians who would fain have prevented that mighty drain of treasure and of the best blood of England- holding, with John Bright, that this war was "neither just nor necessary"; but they were "whistling against the wind." There was one rich English quaker, with a heart like a tender woman's and a face like a cherub's, who actually went over to Russia to labor with "friend Nicholas" against this war. All in vain! the Czar was deeply moved, of course, but would not give in, or give up.

On the 3d of March the Queen went to Parliament to receive the address of both Houses in answer to her message which announced the opening of the war. On this important occasion the young Prince of Wales took a place for the first time with his mother and father on the throne. He looked taller and graver than usual. His heart glowed with martial fire. His voice, too, if he had been allowed to speak, would have been all for war. A few days before this, the Queen, after seeing off the first division of troops for the Baltic, had so felt the soldier-blood of her father tingling in her veins, that she wrote: "I am very enthusiastic about my dear army and navy, and I wish I had two sons in both now." But in later years the widowed Queen is said to have been not eager to have any of her sons, *his* sons, peril their lives in battle.

Though the Prince of Wales now had assigned to him a more honorable place on the British throne than the British Constitution permitted his father, to occupy, he was still perfectly amenable to that father's authority.

An English gentleman lately told me of an instance of the wise exercise of that authority. The Prince-Consort and his son were riding across a London toll-bridge, the keeper of which, on receiving his toll, respectfully saluted them. Prince Albert courteously inclined his head, touching his hat, but Prince Albert Edward dashed carelessly on, yet only to return a minute after, laughing and blushing, to obey his father's command—"My son, go back and return that man's salute."

The Queen was so enthusiastic that she with pleasure saw launched— indeed, christened herself—a war-vessel bearing the name and likeness of her "dearest Albert"— that humane, amiable, peace-loving man! There was something incongruous in it, as there is in all associations between war and good peace-lovers and Christ-lovers.

Amid these wars and rumors of wars, it is comforting to read in that admirable and most comprehensive work, "The Life of His Royal Highness, the Prince-Consort, by Sir Theodore Martin, K.C.B.," of pleasant little domestic events, like a children's May-day ball at Buckingham Palace, given on Prince Arthur's birthday, when two hundred children were made happy and made others happier. Then there were great times at Osborne for the Royal children on their mother's birthday, when a charming house—the Swiss cottage—and its grounds, were made over to them, to have and to hold, as their very own. It was not wholly for a play-house and play- ground, but partly as a means of instruction in many things. In the perfectly-appointed kitchen of the cottage the little Princesses learned to perform many domestic tasks, and to cook different kinds of plain dishes as well as cakes and tarts—in short, to perform the ordinary duties of housekeepers; while in the grounds and gardens the young Princes used to work two or three hours a day under the direction of a gardener, getting regular certificates of labor performed, which they presented to their father, who always paid them as he would have paid any laborer for the same amount and quality of work—never more, never less. Each boy had his own hoe and spade, which not a Princeling among them all considered it *infra-dig.* to use. The two eldest boys, Albert Edward and Alfred, also constructed under their father's directions a small fortress perfect in all its details. All the work on this military structure, even to the making of the bricks, was done by the Princes. The little Princesses also worked in the gardens, each having her own plot, marked with her own name, from Victoria to Beatrice. There was a museum of natural history attached to the cottage, and we can easily imagine the wonderful specimens of entomology and ornithology there to be found. Ah! have any of the grown-up Royal Highnesses ever known the comfort and fun in their grand palaces that they had in the merry old Swiss cottage days?

In the autumn of 1854 Prince Albert went over to Boulogne for a little friendly visit to England's chief ally, taking with him little Arthur. He seems to have found the French Emperor a little stiff and cold at first, as he wrote to the Queen, "The Emperor thaws

75

more and more." In the sunshine of that genial presence he had to thaw. The Prince adds: "He told me one of the deepest impressions ever made upon him was when he arrived in London shortly after King William's death and saw you at the age of eighteen going to open Parliament for the first time."

The Prince made a deep impression on the Emperor. Two men could not be more unlike. The character of the one was crystal clear, and deeper than it appeared—the character of the other was murky and mysterious, and shallower than it seemed.

This must have been a season of great anxiety and sadness for the Queen. The guns of Alma and Sebastopol echoed solemnly among her beloved mountains. In her journal there is this year only one Balmoral entry—not the account of any Highland expedition or festivity, but the mention of an eloquent sermon by the Rev. Norman McLeod, and of his prayer, which she says was "very touching," and added, "His allusions to us were so simple, saying after his mention of us, 'Bless their children.' It gave me a lump in my throat, as also when he prayed for the dying, the wounded, the widow, and the orphan."

There came a few months later a ghastly ally of the Russians into the fight—cholera—which, joined to the two terrible winter months, "Generals January and February," as the Czar called them, made sad havoc in the English and French forces, but did not redeem the fortunes of the Russians. Much mal-administration in regard to army supplies brought terrible hardships upon the English troops, and accomplished the impossible in revealing in them new qualities of bravery and heroic endurance.

It was an awful war, and it lasted as long as, and a little longer than, the Czar, who died in March, 1855. "of pulmonary apoplexy," it was announced, though the rumor ran, that, resolved not to survive Sebastopol, he had taken his own unhappy life. With his death the war was virtually ended, and his son Alexander made peace as soon as he decently could with the triumphant enemies of his father.

Through all this distressful time the Queen and the Prince-Consort manifested the deepest sympathy for, as well as pride in, the English soldiers. They had an intense pity for the poor men in the trenches, badly clad and half starved, grand, patient, ill-used, uncomplaining fellows!

"My heart bleeds to think of it," wrote the Prince, of the army administration. He corresponded with Florence Nightingale, and encouraged her in her brave and saintly mission. When the sick and wounded began to arrive, in England both he and the Queen were faithful in visiting them in the hospitals, and Her Majesty had a peculiar sad joy in rewarding the bravest of the brave with the gift of the Crimean medal. In a private letter she gives a description of the touching scene. She says:

"From the highest Prince of the blood to the lowest private, all received the same distinction for the bravest conduct in the severest actions.... Noble fellows! I own I feel for them as though they were my own children.... They were so touched, so pleased! Many, I hear, cried, and they won't hear of giving up their medals to have their names engraved upon them for fear that they may not receive the identical ones put into their hands by me. Several came by in a sadly mutilated state."

One of these heroes, young Sir Thomas Trowbridge, who had had one leg and the foot of the other carried away by a round shot at Inkermann, was dragged in a Bath-chair to the Queen, who, when she gave him his medal, offered to make him one of her *Aides-de-Camp*, to which the gallant and loyal soldier replied, "I am amply repaid for everything." Poor fellow! I wonder if he continued to say that all his mutilated life?

Whenever during this war there was a hitch, or halt, in the victorious march of English arms, any disaster or disgrace in the Crimea, the attacks upon the Prince-Consort were renewed,—there were even threats of impeachment;—but when the "cruel war was over," the calumnies were over also. They were always as absurd as unfounded. Aside from his manly sense of honor the Prince had by that time, at least, ten good reasons for being loyal to England—an English wife and nine English children.

CHAPTER XXIV.

The Emperor and Empress of France visit Windsor—They are entertained by the City of London—Scene at the Opera—The Queen returns the Emperor's call—Splendor of the Imperial Hospitality.

The Queen's kind heart was really pained by the sudden death of the Czar, her sometime friend and "brother"—whose visit to Windsor was brought by the startling event vividly to her mind—yet she turned from his august shade to welcome one of his living conquerors, the Emperor Napoleon, who, with his beautiful wife, came this spring to visit her and the Prince. She had had prepared for the visitors the most splendid suite of apartments—among them the very bedroom once occupied by the Emperor Nicholas. It was the best "spare room" of the Castle, and the one generally allotted to first-class monarchs—Louis Philippe had occupied it. What stuff for ghosts for the bedside of Louis Napoleon did he and the Czar supply! A few days before the Emperor and Empress arrived, the Queen had a visit from the poor ex-Queen, Marie Amélie. There is a touching entry in Her Majesty's diary, regarding this visit. By the way, I would state that whenever I quote from Her Majesty's diary, it is through the medium of Sir Theodore Martin's book, and by his kind permission.

The Queen wrote: "It made us both so sad to see her drive away in a plain coach, with miserable post-horses, and to think that this was the Queen of the French, and that six years ago her husband was surrounded by the same pomp and grandeur which three days hence would surround his successor."

There is something exquisitely tender and pitiful in this. Most people, royal or republican, would "consider it not so deeply." The world has grown so familiar with the see-saw of French royalty, that a fall or a flight, exile or abdication moves it but little. In the old *guillotine* times, there *were* sensations.

England's great ally, and his lovely wife, Eugénie,—every inch an Empress,—were received with tremendous enthusiasm. Their passage through London was one long ovation. The Times of that date gives allowing account of the crowds and the excitement. It states also, that as they were passing King Street, the Emperor "was observed to draw the attention of the Empress to the house which he had occupied in former days,"—respectable lodgings, doubtless, but how different from the Tuileries!

The Queen gives an interesting account of what seemed a long, and was an impatient waiting for her guests, whom the Prince-Consort had gone to meet. At length, they saw "the advanced guard of the escort—then the cheers of the crowd broke forth. The outriders appeared—the doors opened, I stepped out, the children close behind me; the band struck up '*Partant pour la Syrie*,' the trumpets sounded, and the open carriage, with the Emperor and Empress, Albert sitting opposite them, drove up and they got out... I advanced and embraced the Emperor, who received two salutes on either cheek from me—having first kissed my hand." The English Queen did not do things by halves, any more than the English people. She then embraced the Empress, whom she describes as "very gentle and graceful, but evidently very nervous." The children were then presented, "Vicky, with alarmed eyes, making very low curtsies," and Bertie having the honor of an embrace from the Emperor. Then they all went up-stairs, Prince. Albert conducting the Empress, who at first modestly declined to precede the Queen. Her Majesty followed on the arm of the Emperor, who proudly informed her that he had once been in her service as special constable against those unstable enemies, the Chartists.

The Queen and Prince soon came to greatly like the Emperor and admire the Empress. The Queen wrote of the former: "He is very quiet and amiable, and easy to get on with… Nothing can be more civil and well-bred than the Emperor's manner—so full of tact."

Of Eugenie she wrote: "She is full of courage and spirit, and yet so gentle, with such innocence; … with all her great liveliness, she has the prettiest and most modest manner." Later, Her Majesty, with a rare generosity, showing that there was not room in her large heart even, for any petty feeling, wrote in her private diary, of that beautiful and brilliant woman: "I am delighted to see how much Albert likes and admires her."

There was a State-ball at Windsor, at which Eugénie shone resplendent. The Queen danced with the Emperor—and with her imaginative mind, found cause for wondering reflection in the little circumstance, for she says: "How strange to think that I, the granddaughter of George III., should dance with the Emperor Napoleon III.—nephew of England's greatest enemy, now my dearest and most intimate ally—in the *Waterloo Room*, and this ally only six years ago, living in this country an exile, poor and unthought of!"

The Queen, of course, invested the Emperor with the Order of the Garter. It has been in its time bestowed on monarchs less worthy the honor. It is true, he did not come very heroically by his imperial crown—but when crowns are lying about loose, who can blame a man for helping himself?

The city gave the Emperor and Empress a great reception and banquet at Guildhall, and in the evening there was a memorable visit to the opera. The imperial and royal party drove from Buckingham Palace through a dense crowd and illuminated streets. Arrived at the royal box, the Queen took the Emperor by the hand, and smiling her sweetest—which is saying a good deal—presented him to the audience. Immense enthusiasm! Then Prince Albert led forward the lovely Empress, and the enthusiasm was unbounded. It must be that this still beautiful, though sorrowful woman, on whose head a fierce tempest of misfortune has beaten—the most piteous, discrowned, blanched head since Marie Antoinette—sometimes remembers those happy and glorious days, and that the two august widows talk over them together.

At last came the hour of farewells, and the Emperor departed with his pretty, tearful wife—the band playing his mother's air, *Partant pour la Syrie*, and his heart full of pride and gratitude. In a letter which he addressed to the Queen, soon after reaching home, is revealed one cause of his gratitude. After saying many pleasant things about the kind and gracious reception which had been accorded him, and the impression which the sight of the happy home-life of Windsor had made upon him, he says: "Your Majesty has also touched me to the heart by the delicacy of the consideration shown to the Empress; for nothing pleases more than to see the person one loves become the object of such flattering attention."

That summer there appeared among the royal children at Osborne a sudden illness, which soon put on royal livery, and was recognized as scarlet fever. There was, of course, great alarm—but nothing very serious came of it. The two elder children escaped the infection, and were allowed to go to Paris with their parents, who in July returned the visit of the Emperor and Empress. They went in their yacht to Boulogne, where the Emperor met them and escorted them to the railway on horseback. He looked best, almost handsome, on horseback. Arrived at Paris, they found the whole city decorated, as only the French know how to decorate, and gay, enthusiastic crowds cheering, as only the French know how to cheer. They drove through splendid boulevards, through the Bois de Boulogne, over the bridge, to the Palace of St. Cloud—and everywhere there were the imperial troops, artillery, cavalry and zouaves, their bands playing "God Save the Queen." Those only who knew Paris under the Empire, can realize what that reception was, and how magnificent were the *fêtes* and how grand the reviews of the next ten days.

78

Of the arrival at St. Cloud the Queen writes: "In all the blaze of light from lamps and torches, amidst the roar of cannon and bands and drums and cheers, we reached the palace. The Empress, with the Princess Mathilde and the ladies, received us at the door, and took us up a beautiful staircase, lined with the splendid *Cent-Guardes,* who are magnificent men, very like our Life Guards... We went through the rooms at once to our own, which are charming... I felt quite bewildered, but enchanted, everything is so beautiful."

This palace we know was burned during the siege. The last time I visited the ruins, I stood for some minutes gazing through a rusty grating into the noble vestibule, through which so many royal visitors had passed. Its blackened walls and broken and prostrate marbles are overspread by a wild natural growth—a green shroud wrapping the ghastly ruin;—or rather, it was like an incursion of a mob of rough vegetation, for there were neither delicate ferns, nor poetic ivy, but democratic grass and republican groundsel and communistic thistles and nettles. In place of the splendid *Cent-Guardes* stood tall, impudent weeds; in place of courtiers, the supple and bending briar; while up the steps, which the Queen and Empress and their ladies ascended that night, pert little *grisettes* of *marguerites* were climbing.

So perfect was the hospitality of the Emperor that they had things as English as possible at the Palace-even providing an English chaplain for Sunday morning. In the afternoon, however, he backslid into French irreligion and natural depravity, and they all went to enjoy the fresh air, the sight of the trees, the flowers and the children in the Bois de Boulogne. The next day they went into the city to the *Exposition des Beaux Arts,* and to the *Elysée* for lunch and a reception—then they all drove to the lovely *Sainte Chapelle* and the *Palais de Justice*. There the Emperor pointed out the old *Conciergerie,* and said—"There is where I was imprisoned." Doubtless he thought that was a more interesting historical fact than the imprisonment of poor Marie Antoinette, in the same grim building. There was also a visit to the Italian opera, where a very pretty surprise awaited the guests. At the close of the ballet, the scene suddenly changed to a view of Windsor—including the arrival of the Emperor and Empress. "*God Save the Queen*" was sung superbly, and rapturously applauded. One day the Queen, Prince, and Princess Royal, dressed very plainly, took a hired carriage and had a long *incognito* drive through Paris. They enjoyed this "lark" immensely. Then there was a grand ball at the *Hotel de Ville*, and a grand review on the *Champ de Mars*, and a visit by torchlight to the tomb of *the* Napoleon, under the dome of the *Invalides*, with the accompaniment of solemn organ-playing within the church, and a grand midsummer storm outside, with thunder and lightning. The French do so well understand how to manage these things!

The grandest thing of all was a State ball in Versailles;—that magnificent but mournful, almost monumental pile, being gaily decorated and illuminated—almost transformed out of its tragic traditions. What a charming picture of her hostess the Queen gives us:

"The Empress met us at the top of the staircase, looking like a fairy queen, or nymph, in a white dress, trimmed with grass and diamonds,—a beautiful *tour de corsage* of diamonds round the top of her dress;—the same round her waist, and a corresponding *coiffure*, with her Spanish and Portuguese orders."

She must have been a lovely vision. The Emperor thought so, for (according to the Queen) forgetting that it is not "good form" for a man to admire or compliment his own wife, he exclaimed, as she appeared: "*Comme tu es belle!* " ("How beautiful you are!")

I am afraid he was not always so polite. During her first season at the Tuileries, which she called "a beautiful prison," and which is now as much a thing of the past as the Bastile, she often in her gay, impulsive way offended against the stern laws of Court etiquette, and was reproved for a lack of dignity. Once at a reception she suddenly perceived a little way down the line an old school-friend, and, hurrying forward, kissed her affectionately. It was nice for the young lady, but the Emperor frowned and said, in that cold marital tone which cuts like an east wind: "Madame, you forget that you are the Empress!"

In a letter from the Prince to his uncle Leopold I find this suggestive sentence in reference to the ball at Versailles: "Victoria made her toilette in Marie Antoinette's boudoir." It would almost seem the English Queen might have feared to see in her dressing-glass a vision of the French Queen's proud young head wearing a diadem as brilliant as her own, or perhaps that cruel crown of silver—her terror-whitened hair.

The parting was sad. The Empress "could not bring herself to face it"; so the Queen went to her room with the Emperor, who said: "Eugénie, here is the Queen." "Then," adds Her Majesty, "she came and gave me a beautiful fan and a rose and heliotrope from the garden, and Vicky a bracelet set with rubies and diamonds containing her hair, with which Vicky was delighted."

The Emperor went with them all the way to Boulogne and saw them on board their yacht; then came embracings and *adieux*, and all was over.

The next morning early they reached Osborne and were received at the beach by Prince Alfred and his little brothers, to whom Albert Edward, big with the wonders of Paris, was like a hero out of a fairy book. Near the house waited the sisters, Helena and Louise, and in the house the invalid—"poor, dear Alice!"—for whom the joy of that return was almost too much.

CHAPTER XXV.

Betrothal of the Princess Royal—Birth of the Prince Imperial of France— More visitors and visitings—The Emperor And Empress of Mexico—Marriage of the Princess Royal—The attendant festivities.

At Balmoral, where they took possession of the new Castle, the Queen and Prince received the news of the approaching fall of Sebastopol, for it was not down yet. It finally fell amid a scene of awful conflagration and explosions—the work of the desperate Russians themselves.

The peace-rejoicings did not come till later, but in the new house at Balmoral there was a new joy, though one not quite unmixed with sadness, in the love and happy betrothal of the Princess Victoria. In her journal the Queen tells the old, old story very quietly: "Our dear Victoria was this day engaged to Prince Frederick William of Prussia. He had already spoken to us of his wishes, but were uncertain, on account of her extreme youth, whether he should speak to her or wait till he should come back again. However, we felt it was better he should do so, and, during our ride up Craig-na-Ban this afternoon; he picked a piece of white heather (the emblem of good luck), which he gave to her." This it seems broke the ice, and so the poetic Prince (all German Princes, except perhaps Bismarck, are poetic and romantic) told his love and offered his hand, which was not rejected. Then came a few weeks of courtship, doubtless as bright and sweet to the royal pair of lovers as was a similar season to Robert Burns and "Highland Mary"—for love levels up and levels down— and then young Fritz returned to Germany, leaving behind him a fond heart and a tearful little face round and fair.

From this time till the marriage of the Princess Royal, which was not till after her seventeenth birthday in 1858, the Prince-Consort devoted himself more and more to the education of this beloved daughter—in history, art, literature, and religion. He conversed much and most seriously with her in preparation for her confirmation. He found that this work of mental and moral development was "its own exceeding great reward."

The character of the Princess Royal seems to have been in some respects like that of the Princess Charlotte of Wales. She was as high-spirited, strong-willed, gay, free, and fearless; but with infinitely better and purer domestic and social influences, she grew up into a nobler and more gracious young womanhood. Intellectually and morally, she was her father's creation; intellectually and morally, poor Princess Charlotte was worse than fatherless.

But I must hurry on with the hurrying years. The Prince, writing to Baron Stockmar in March, 1856, says: "The telegraph has just brought the news of the Empress having been safely delivered of a son. Great will be the rejoicing in the Tuileries."

This baby born in the purple was the Prince Imperial, whose fate beggars tragedy; who went to gather laurels on an African desert and fell a victim to a savage ambuscade—his beautiful body stuck almost as full of cruel darts as that of the martyred young St. Sebastian.

On March 21st the long-delayed treaty of peace was signed. After all the waste, the agony, the bloodshed, the Prince wrote: "It is not such as we could have wished." But he had learned to bear these little disappointments.

Prince Alfred began his studies for the navy. Fritz of Prussia came over on a visit to his betrothed, and his father and mother soon followed— coming to get better acquainted with their daughter-in-law to be. Then into the royal circle there came another royal guest, all unbidden—the king whose name is Death. The Prince of Leiningen—the Queen's half- brother in blood, but whole brother in heart—died, to her great grief; and soon after there passed away her beloved aunt, the Duchess of Gloucester, a good and amiable woman, and the last of the fifteen children of George the Third and Queen Charlotte. But here life balanced death, for on April 14th another daughter was born in Buckingham Palace. The Prince in a letter to his step-mother speaks of the baby as "thriving famously, and prettier than babies usually are." He adds, "Mama—Aunt, Vicky and her bridegroom are to be the little one's sponsors, and she is to receive the historical, romantic, euphonious, and melodious names of Beatrice Mary Victoria Feodora."

That summer there came two very interesting royal visitors to Windsor— the young Princess Charlotte of Belgium and her betrothed husband, the Archduke Maximilian of Austria. Prince Albert wrote of the young girl: "Charlotte's whole being seems to me to have been warmed and unfolded by the love which is kindled in her heart." To his uncle Leopold he wrote:" I wish you joy at having got such a husband for dear Charlotte, as I am sure he is quite worthy of her and will make her happy."

Just ten years from that time the Emperor Maximilian, standing before a file of Mexican soldiers at Queretaro, took out his watch, which he would never more need, and, pressing a spring, revealed in its case a miniature of the lovely Empress Charlotte, which he kissed tenderly. Then, handing the watch to the priest at his side, he said: "Carry this souvenir to my dear wife in Europe, and if she ever be able to understand you, say that my eyes closed with the impression of her image, which I shall carry with me above."

She never did understand. She lives in a phantom Court, believing herself still Empress of Mexico, and that the Emperor will soon come home from the wars to her and the throne.

There was this summer a memorable show in Hyde Park, when Queen Victoria on horseback, in her becoming military dress, pinned with her own hands on to the coats of a large number of heroes of the great war the coveted Victoria Cross. Ah! they were proud and she was prouder. She is a true soldier's daughter; her heart always thrills at deeds of valor and warms at sight of a hero, however humble.

The Prince went over to his cousin Charlotte's wedding, and the Queen, compelled to stay behind, wrote to King Leopold that her letting her husband, go without her was a great proof of her love for her uncle. "You cannot think," she said, "how completely forlorn I feel when he is away, or how I count the hours till he returns. All the children are as nothing when he is away. It seems as if the whole life of the house and home were gone."

Again, how like a loving Scotch peasant wife:

"There's na luck about the house,
There's na luck at a'—
   There's little pleasure in the house,
When my guid mon's awa'."

In August the Emperor and Empress made a flying visit in their yacht to Osborne and talked over the latest political events, the new phases of affairs, and, doubtless, the new babies; and, a little later, the Queen and Prince ran over to Cherbourg in their yacht, taking six of the children. There was a perfect nursery of the little ones, "rocked in the cradle of the deep." This was such a complete "surprise party," that the Emperor and Empress away in Paris, knew nothing about it. They all took a pleasant little excursion into the lovely country of Normandy in *chars-à-bancs*, with bells on the post-horses, doubtless, and everything gay and delightful and novel to the children,—especially French sunshine.

This year the Balmoral stay was greatly saddened by the news of the Sepoy rebellion, of the tragedies of Cawnpore, and the unspeakable atrocities of Nana Sahib. Young people nowadays know little about that ghastly war, except as connected with the pretty poetical story of the relief of Lucknow, and Jessie Brown; but, at the time, it was an awfully real thing, and not in the least poetical or romantic.

The marriage of the Princess Royal was fixed for January 25, 1858. Her father wrote from Balmoral hi the autumn; "Vicky suffers under the feeling that every spot she visits she has to greet for the last time as home... The departure from here will, be a great trial to us all, especially to Vicky, who leaves it for good and all; and the good, simple Highlanders, who are very fond of us, are constantly saying to her, and often with tears, 'I suppose we shall never see you again?' which naturally makes her feel more keenly."

At last the wedding day approached and the royal guests began to arrive at Buckingham Palace, and they poured in till on fair days a King or Queen, a Prince or Princess looked out of nearly every window; and when there was a fog, collisions of crowned heads occurred in the corridors. On the day the Court left Windsor the Queen wrote: "Went to look at the rooms prepared for Vicky's honeymoon; very pretty... We took a short walk with Vicky, who was dreadfully upset at this real break in her life; the real separation from her childhood."

These be little things perhaps, but beautiful little human things, showing the warm love and tender sympathy which united this family, supposed to be lifted high and dry above ordinary humanity, among the arid and icy grandeurs of royalty.

There was a gay little ball one evening with Highnesses and Serenities dancing and whirling and chasséing, and a "*grande chaine*" of half of the sovereigns of Europe—all looking very much like other people. The Queen wrote: "Ernest (Duke of Coburg) said it seemed like a dream to see Vicky dance as a bride, just as I did eighteen years ago, and I still (so he said) looking very young. In 1840, poor dear papa (late Duke of Coburg) danced with me as Ernest danced with Vicky."

Afterwards there was a grand ball, attended by over a thousand of the elect, and for the multitude there were dramatic and musical entertainments. At Her Majesty's Theatre one night the famous tragedian, Mr. Phelps, and the great actress, Miss Helen Faucit, in the tragedy of *Macbeth*, froze the blue blood of a whole tier of royal personages and made them realize what crowns were worth, and how little they had earned theirs, by showing what men and women will go through with to secure one. The Emperor and Empress of France were not among the guests. They had been a little upset by an event more tragic than are most marriages—the attempt of Orsini to blow up their carriage, by the explosion of hand-grenades near the entrance of the Italian Opera. They had been only slightly hurt, but some eighty innocent people in the crowd had been either killed or wounded. The white dress of the Empress was sprinkled with blood, yet she went to her box and sat out the performance. What nerve these imperial people have!

The Queen's account of this glad, sad time of the marriage is very natural, moving and maternal. First, there was the domestic and Court sensation of the arrival of the bridegroom, Prince "Fritz," whom the Prince-Consort had gone to meet, and all the Court awaited. "I met him," says the Queen, "at the bottom of the staircase, very warmly; he was pale and nervous. At the top of the staircase Vicky received him, with Alice." That afternoon all the royal people witnessed a grand dramatic performance of "Taming the Horse," with Mr. Rarey as "leading man." In the evening they went to the opera. The next day, Sunday, the presents were shown—a marvelous collection of jewels, plate, lace and India shawls, and they had service and listened to a sermon. It is wonderful what these great people can get through with! Coming in from a walk they found a lot of new presents added to the great pile. The Queen writes: "Dear Vicky gave me a brooch, a very pretty one, containing her hair, and clasping me in her arms, said,' I hope to be worthy to be your child.'"

From all I hear I should say that fond hope has been realized in a noble and beneficent life. The Crown Princess of Germany is a woman greatly loved and honored.

On the wedding day the Queen wrote: "The second most eventful day of my life, as regards feelings; I felt as if I were being married over again myself... While dressing, dearest Vicky came in to see me, looking well and composed."

The Princess Royal, like her mother, was married in the Chapel of St. James' Palace, and things went on very much as on that memorable wedding day—always spoken of by the Queen as "blessed." She now could describe more as a spectator the shouting, the bell-ringing, the cheering and trumpetings, and the brave sight of the procession. Prince Albert and King Leopold and "the two eldest boys went first. Then the three girls (Alice, Helena and Louise), in pink satin, lace and flowers." There were eight bridesmaids in "white tulle, with wreaths and bouquets of roses and white heather." That was a pretty idea, using the simple betrothal flower of the Prince and Princess-for "luck."

The Queen speaks of "Mama looking so handsome in violet velvet; trimmed with ermine." Ah, the young Victoria was the only daughter of *her* Victoria, who as a bride was to receive on her brow that grandmother's kiss—dearer and holier than any priestly benediction. I like to read that immediately after the ceremony the bride "kissed her grandmama."

After the wedding breakfast at the Palace the bridal pair, Victoria and Frederick William, drove away just as eighteen years before Victoria and Albert had driven away—the same state, the same popular excitement, in kind if not in degree, and, let us trust, a like amount of love and joy. But this happy pair did not drive all the way to Windsor. The waiting train, the iron horse snorting with impatience, showed how the world had moved on since that other wedding; but the perennial Eton boys were on hand for these lovers also, wearing the same tall hats and short jackets, cheering in the same mad way, so that the Queen herself would hardly have suspected them to be the other boys' sons, or younger brothers. They "scored one" above their honored predecessors by dragging the carriage from the Windsor station to the Castle.

The Court soon followed to Windsor with thirty-five of the royal guests, and there were banquets and more investings, till it would seem that the Queen's stock of jeweled garters must be running low. Then back to town for more presents and operas and plays, and addresses of congratulation, and at last came the dismal morning of separation. The day

83

before, the Queen had written: "The last day of our dear child being with us, which is incredible, and makes me feel at times quite sick at heart." She records that that poor child exclaimed, "I think it will kill me to take leave of dear papa!"

The next morning, she writes," Vicky came with a very sad face to my room. Here we embraced each other tenderly, and our tears flowed fast."

Then there were leave-takings from the loving grandmama and the younger brothers and sisters ("Bertie" and Alfred going with their father to Gravesend, to see the bridal party embarked), and hardest of all, the parting of the child from the mother.

To quote again: "A dreadful moment and a dreadful day! Such sickness came over me—real heart-ache,—when I thought of our dearest child being gone, and for so long... It began to snow before Vicky went, and continued to do so without intermission all day."

In spite of the dreary weather, I am told that thousands of London people were assembled in the streets to catch a last glimpse of the popular Princess Royal. They could hardly recognize her pleasant, rosy, child- like face—it was so sad, so swollen with weeping. They did not then look with much favor on the handsome Prussian Prince at her side—and one loyal Briton shouted out, "If he doesn't treat you well, come back to us!" That made her laugh. I believe he did treat her well, and that she has been always happy as a wife, though for a time she is said to have fretted against the restraints of German Court etiquette, which bristled all round her. She found that the straight and narrow ways of that princely paradise were not hedged with roses, as at home, but with briars. Some she respected, and some she bravely broke through.

The little bride was most warmly received in her new home, and about the anniversary of her own marriage-day, the Queen had the happiness of receiving from her new son this laconic telegram: "The whole royal family is enchanted with my wife. F. W."

Afterwards, in writing to her uncle, of her daughter's success at the Prussian Court, and of her happiness, the Queen says: "But her heart often yearns for home and those she loves dearly—above all, her dear papa, for whom she has *un culte* (a worship) which is touching and delightful to see."

Her father returned this "worship" by tenderness and devotion unfailing and unwearying. His letters to the Crown Princess are perhaps the sweetest and noblest, most thoughtful and finished of his writings. They show that he respected as well as loved his correspondent, of whom, indeed, he had spoken to her husband as one having "a man's head and a child's heart." His letters to his uncle and the Baron are full of his joy, intellectual and affectional, in this his first-born daughter; but the last-born was not forgotten. In one letter he writes: "Little Beatrice is an extremely attractive, pretty, intelligent child; indeed, the most amusing baby we have had." Again—"Beatrice on her first birthday looks charming, with a new light-blue cap. Her table of birthday gifts has given her the greatest pleasure; especially a lamb."

I know these are little, common domestic bits—that is just why I cull them out of grave letters, full of great affairs of State.

CHAPTER XXVI.

Visiting and counter-visiting—Charming domestic gossip—The Queen's first grandchild—The Prince of Wales' trip to America—Another love- affair—Death of the Duchess of Kent.

In May, Prince Albert ran over to Germany to visit his old home, and his new son, and his darling daughter, whom he found well and happy. In one of his letters to the Queen from Gotha, he says: "I enclose a forget-me- not from grandmama's grave."

There is in that simple sentence an exquisite indication of his affectionate and constant nature. This was a hurried visit, with many interests and excitements, and yet the grave of that infirm, deaf, old Dowager Duchess, who had, as practical people say, "outlived her usefulness," was not found "out of the way." There was little need of the dear grandmama calling softly through that tender blue flower— "*Vergiss mein nicht, mein Engel Albert!*" He never forgot.

In July, the Queen and Prince took to their yacht again, for a visit to the Emperor and Empress, at Cherbourg, and had a grand reception, and there was a great *fête*, and fireworks and bombs and rockets; but the account is not half so interesting to me as the one given by Her Majesty, of their return to Osborne; an exquisite picture that, which I feel I must reproduce almost entire: ... "At twenty minutes to five, we landed at our peaceful Osborne. ... The evening was very warm and calm. Dear Affie was on the pier, and we found all the other children, including Baby, standing at the door. Deckel (a favorite dog), and our new charming kennel-bred Dachs 'Boy,' also received us with joy." I like that bringing in of the dogs to complete the-picture.

The Queen continues: "We went to see Affie's (Alfred's) table of birthday presents— entirely nautical. ... We went with the children, Alice and I driving, to the Swiss Cottage, which was all decked out with flags in honor of Affie's birthday. ... I sat (at dinner) between Albert and Affie. The two little boys (Princes Arthur and Leopold) appeared. A band played, and after dinner we danced, with the three boys and three girls, a merry country dance on the terrace."

A little later, the Queen and Prince made a visit to their daughter in Germany. Her Majesty's description of the happy meeting is very sweet. "There on the platform stood our darling child, with a nosegay in her hand. She stepped in, and long and warm, was the embrace. ... So much to say and to tell and ask, yet so unaltered—looking well—quite the old Vicky still."

From beautiful Babelsberg, she wrote: "Vicky came and sat with me. I felt as if she were my own again."

This was not a long, but a very happy visit; the Queen and Prince had received many courteous attentions from the Prussian Court, and had found their beloved daughter proud and content. From Osborne, in a letter to his daughter, the Prince-Consort writes: "Alfred looks very nice and handsome in his new naval cadet's uniform—the round-jacket and the long- tailed coat, with the broad knife by his side." The next month the Prince went to Spithead, to see this son off on a two-years' cruise—and felt that his family had indeed begun to break up. The next exciting public matter was the news of Louis Napoleon's alliance with King Victor Emmanuel in the war against Austria. And this was the Emperor who, had given out that his empire was "peace"—that the only clang of arms henceforth to be heard therein would be a mighty beating of swords and spears into plow-shares and pruning-hooks. The next domestic excitement was caused by a telegram from Berlin, announcing the birth of a son to the Crown Prince and Princess, and that mother and child were doing well. Queen Victoria was a grandmother, and prouder, I doubt not, than when afterwards she was made Empress of India.

For her mother's birthday, in May, 1859, the Crown Princess came over and made a delightful little visit. The Queen wrote of her: "Dear Vicky is a charming companion." Of the Princess Alice she had before written: "She is very good, sensible and amiable, and a real comfort to me." Mothers know how much there is in those words—"a real comfort to me." The Crown Princess found most change in baby—Beatrice—and after her return home, her father often wrote to her of this little sister: "The little aunt," he says, "makes daily progress, and is really too comical. When she tumbles, she calls out, in bewilderment, 'She don't like it! She don't like it!'—and she-came into breakfast a short time ago, with her eyes full of tears, moaning, 'Baby has been so naughty,—poor baby so naughty!' as one might complain of being ill, or of having slept badly." Later in the year the Prince writes: "Alice comes out admirably, and is a great support to her mother.

85

Lenchen (the Princess Helena) is very distinguished, and little Arthur amiable and full of promise as ever."

In November, Prince Frederick William and his Princess came over on a visit—and the fond father wrote: "Vicky has developed greatly of late— and yet remains quite a child; of such, indeed, 'is the kingdom of heaven.'" Of the Prince he said: "He has quite delighted us." So all was right then. About this time he said of his daughter, Alice, that she had become "a handsome young woman, of graceful form and presence, and is a help and stay to us all in the house." What a rich inheritance such praise!

In the Queen's diary there was, on July 24, 1860, an interesting entry: "Soon after we sat down to breakfast came a telegram from Fritz—Vicky had got a daughter, at 8:10, and both doing well! What joy! Children jumping about, every one delighted—so thankful and relieved."

The Prince wrote to his daughter as only *he* could write—wisely and thoughtfully, yet tenderly and brightly. There was in this letter a charming passage about his playfellow, Beatrice. After saying of his new grandchild, "The little girl must be a darling," he adds, "Little girls are much prettier than boys. I advise her to model herself after her Aunt Beatrice. That excellent lady has now not a moment to spare. 'I have no time,' she says, when she is asked for anything, 'I must write letters to my niece.'"

Shortly after his first little niece was born, the Prince of Wales made his first acquaintance with the New World. He went over to America to visit the vast domain which was to be his, some day, and the vaster domain which might have been his, but for the blind folly of his great- grandfather, George III. and his Ministers, who, like the rash voyagers of the "Arabian Nights' Entertainment," kindled a fire on the back of a whale, thinking it "solid land," till the leviathan "put itself in motion," and flung them and their "merchandise" off into the sea. He was a fine young fellow, the Prince, and was received with loyal enthusiasm, and heartily liked in the Canadas. I believe we of the States treated him very well, also—and that he had what Americans call "a good time," dancing with pretty girls in the Eastern cities, and shooting prairie- chickens on the Western plains. I think we did not overdo the matter in fêting and following the son of the beloved Queen of England. We had other business on hand just then—a momentous Presidential election—the election of Abraham Lincoln.

In our capital he was treated to a ball, a visit to the Patent-Office and the tomb of Washington, and such like gaieties. President Buchanan entertained him as handsomely as our national palace, the White House, would allow; and afterwards wrote a courtly letter to Queen Victoria, congratulating her on the charming behavior of her son and heir—"*the expectancy and rose of the fair State*." The Queen replied very graciously and even gratefully, addressing Mr. Buchanan as "my good friend." That was the most she could do, according to royal rules. The elected temporary ruler of our great American empire, even should it become greater by the annexation of Cuba and Mexico, can never expect to be addressed as "*mon frère*" by regularly born, bred, crowned and anointed sovereigns—or even by a reigning Prince or Grand Duke; can never hope to be embraced and kissed on both cheeks by even the Prince of Monaco, the King of the Sandwich Islands, or the Queen of Madagascar. We must make up our minds to that.

In the early autumn of 1860, the Queen, Prince, and Princess Alice went over to Germany for another sight of their dear ones. It was the last visit that the Queen was to pay with the Prince to his beloved fatherland. They were delighted with their grandson, and I hope with their granddaughter also. Of baby Wilhelm the Queen writes: "Such a little love. ... He is a fine, fat child, with a beautiful, soft white skin, very fine shoulders and limbs, and a very dear face. ... He has Fritz's eyes and Vicky's mouth, and very fair, curling hair." Afterwards she wrote: "Dear little William came to me, as he does every morning. He is such a darling, so intelligent."

86

I believe this darling grandchild was the "little love" who gave to the Queen her first great-grandchild.

At Coburg the Prince-Consort came frightfully near being killed by the running away of his carriage-horses. The accident was a great shock to the Queen, and the escape an unspeakable joy. At Mayence Her Majesty confided a family secret to her discreet diary. During a visit from the Prince and Princess Charles of Hesse-Darmstadt it was settled that the young Prince Louis should come to England to get better acquainted with the Princess Alice, whom he already greatly admired. So everything was arranged and the way smoothed for these lovers, and in this case the union proved as happy as though brought about in the usual hap-hazard way of marriages in common life.

The next November the Prince wrote from Windsor: "The Prince Louis of Hesse is here on a visit. The young people seem to like each other. He is very simple, natural, frank and thoroughly manly."

The next day the Queen jotted down in her diary the simple story of the betrothal in a way to reveal how fresh in her own heart was the romance of her youth:

"After dinner, while talking to the gentlemen, I perceived Alice and Louis talking before the fireplace more earnestly than usual, and when I passed to go to the other room both came up to me, and Alice in much agitation said he had proposed to her, and he begged for my blessing. I could only squeeze his hand and say 'Certainly,' and that we would see him in my room later. Got through the evening, working as well as we could. Alice came to our room. ... Albert sent for Louis to his room, then called Alice and me in. ... Louis has a warm, noble heart. We embraced our dear Alice and praised her much to him. He pressed and kissed my hand and I embraced him." The Queen was right, as she generally was in her estimate of character. This son-in-law, of whom she has always been especially fond, is a Prince of amiable and noble disposition, good ability and remarkable cultivation; not exactly a second Prince Albert— *he* was a century plant.

At this Christmas time the Queen's two eldest sons were at home and full of strange stories of strange lands. Soon after, the Prince of Wales went to Cambridge and Prince Alfred joined his ship. Before that cruise was over a deeper, darker sea rolled between the sailor lad and his father.

On February 9, 1861, Prince Albert wrote Baron Stockmar: "To-morrow our marriage will be twenty-one years old. How many storms have swept over it, and still it continues green and fresh." The anniversary occurring on Sunday was very quietly observed, chiefly by the performance in the evening of some fine sacred music, the appropriateness of which was scarcely realized at the time. In a very sweet letter to the Duchess of Kent, such a letter as few married men write to their mothers-in-law, the Prince says: ... "To-day our marriage comes of age, according to law. We have faithfully kept our pledge for better and for worse,' and have only to thank God that He has vouchsafed so much happiness to us. May He have us in His keeping for the days to come! You have, I trust, found good and loving children in us, and we have experienced nothing but love and kindness from you."

This dear "Mama-aunt" had been in delicate health for some time, and once or twice seriously ill, but she seemed better, her physicians were encouraging and all were hopeful till the 12th of March, when the Queen and Prince were suddenly summoned from London to Frogmore by the news of a very alarming relapse. They went at once with all speed, yet the Queen says "the way seemed so long." When they readied the house, the Queen writes: "Albert went up first, and when he returned with tears in his eyes, I saw what awaited me. ... With a trembling heart I went up the staircase and entered the bedroom, and here on a sofa, supported by cushions, sat leaning back my beloved Mama, breathing rather heavily, but in her silk dressing-gown, with her cap on, looking quite herself. ... I knelt before her, kissed her dear hand and placed it next my cheek; but though she opened her eyes she did not, I think, know me. She brushed my hand off, and the dreadful reality was before me that for the first time, she did not know the child she had ever received with such tender smiles."

The further description given by the Queen of this first great sorrow of her life, is exceedingly pathetic and vivid. It is the very poetry of grief. I cannot reproduce it entire, nor give that later story of incalculable loss as related by her in that diary, through which her very heart beats. It is all too unutterably sad. There are passages in this account most exquisitely natural and touching. When all was over, the poor daughter tried to comfort herself with thoughts of the blessed rest of the good mother, of the gentle spirit released from the pain-racked body, but the heart would cry out: "But I—I, wretched child, who had lost the mother I so tenderly loved, from whom for these forty-one years I had never been parted, except for a few weeks, what was my case? My childhood, everything seemed to crowd upon me at once... What I had dreaded and fought—off the idea of, for years, had come, and must be borne... Oh, if I could nave been with her these last weeks! How I grudge every hour I did not spend with her! ... What a blessing we went on Tuesday. The remembrance of her parting blessing, of her dear, sweet smile, will ever remain engraven on my memory."

During all this time, the Queen received the most tender sympathy and care from her children, and Prince Albert, was—*Prince Albert*;— weeping with her, yet striving to comfort her, full of loving kindness and consideration.

The Queen's grief was perhaps excessive, as her love had been beyond measure, but he was not impatient with it, though he writes from Osborne, some weeks after the funeral of the Duchess: "She (the Queen) is greatly upset, and feels her childhood rush back upon her memory with the most vivid force. Her grief is extreme... For the last two years her constant care and occupation have been to keep watch over her mother's comfort, and the influence of this upon her own character has been most salutary. In body she is well, though terribly nervous, and the children are a great disturbance to her. She remains almost entirely alone."

How true to nature! When the first love of a life is suddenly uprooted, all the later growths, however strong, seem to have been torn up with it. When the mother goes, only the child seems to remain. Victoria, tender mother as she herself was, and adoring wife, was now the little girl of Kensington and Claremont, whose little bed was at the side of her mother's, and who had waked to find that mother's bed empty, and forever empty! And yet she said in her first sense of the loss: "I seemed to have lived through a life; to have become old."

We may say that with the coming of that first sorrow went out the youth of the Queen; for it seems that while her mother lives, a woman is always young, that there is something of girlhood, of childhood even, lingering in her life while she can lay her tired head on her mother's knee, or hide her tearful face against her mother's breast, that most sweet and restful refuge from the trials and weariness of life.

Her Majesty's sister, Feodore, strove to comfort her; the dear daughter Victoria came to her almost immediately; her people's tears and prayers were for her, and amid the quiet and seclusion of Osborne she slowly regained her cheerfulness; but the old gladness and content never came back. The children, too, with all the natural gayety of their years, found that something of sweetness and comfort had dropped out of life— something of the charm and dearness of home was gone with "grandmama," from the Palace, the Castle, the seaside mansion, as well as from pleasant Frogmore, where they were always so welcome. Not till then, perhaps, had they known all she was to them—what a blessed element in their lives was her love, so tender and indulgent. Age is necessary to the family completeness. We do not even in our humbler condition, always realize, this—do not see how the quiet waning life in the old arm-chair gives dignity and serenity to the home, till the end comes—till the silver-haired presence is withdrawn.

PART IV.

WIDOWHOOD.

CHAPTER XXVII.

Failing health of Prince Albert—His last visit to Balmoral—His influence upon the policy of England in the *Trent* difficulty with the United States—Strange revolution in English sentiment in respect to American slavery—The setting of the sun.

All this time while the Queen was absorbed by anxious care, or passionate grief for her mother, the health of the Prince-Consort was slowly but surely failing. The keen blade of his active mind was wearing out its sheath. His vital forces must have begun to give out long before actual illness, or he would not so easily have resigned himself to the thought of the long rest,—still young as he was, with so much to enjoy in life, and so much to do. It is said that he had premonitions of early death, and tried to prepare the Queen for his going first—but the realization of a loss so immense could not find lodgment in her mind. Yet though often feeling weak and languid, he did not relax his labors—spurring up his flagging powers. He never lost his interest in public affairs, or in his children's affairs of the heart. He was happy in contemplating the happiness of his daughter Alice, and followed with his heart the journey of his son, Albert Edward, in his visit to the country of the fierce old Vikings, to woo the daughter of a King of another sort—a Princess so fair and fresh that she could

—"*with lilies boast, And with the half-blown rose.*"

That summer his daughter Victoria, with her husband (now Crown Prince) and their children, came again, for a long visit, and there were many other guests, and much was done to cheer the Queen; but her first birthday in orphanage was hopelessly sad, and when that of the Prince came round, his last—though she wrote to her uncle, "This is the dearest of days, and one which fills my heart with love and gratitude," she murmured, because her "beloved mama" was not there to wish him joy. Ah, what an acting, unreasoning thing is the human heart!

Yet the Queen seems to have had a brief return of happiness—to have been upborne on a sudden tide of youthful joyance, during their autumn stay at Balmoral. She wrote: "Being out a good deal here and seeing new and fine scenery does me good." Of their last great Highland excursion, she said: "Have enjoyed nothing so much, or felt so much cheered by anything since my great sorrow."

Because of this intense love of nature—not the holiday, dressed-up nature, of English parks, streams and lakes—but as she appears in all her wildness, ruggedness, raggedness and simple grandeur, in the glorious land of Scott and Burns, the Queen's journal, though a little clouded at the last, by that "great sorrow," is very pleasant, breezy reading. It gives one a breath of heather, and pine and peat-smoke.

After coming from Balmoral, and its bracing outdoor avocations and amusements, the Prince-Consort's health seemed to decline again. He suffered from rheumatic pains and sleeplessness, and he began to feel the chill shadows of the valley he was nearing, creeping around him. The last work of his beneficent life was one of peculiar interest to Americans. It was the amicable arrangement, in conjunction with the Queen, of the ugly affair of the *Trent*. That was a trying time for Americans in England, unless they were of the South, southerly. We of the North, in the beginning of our war for the Union, found to our sad surprise that the sympathies of perhaps the majority of the English were on the side of our opponents. These very people had been ever before, so decidedly and ardently anti-slavery in their sentiments—had counseled such stern and valiant measures for the removal of our "national disgrace," that their new attitude amazed us. We could not understand what sort of a moral whirlwind it was that had caught them up, turned them round, borne them off and set them down on the other side of Mason and Dixon's Line. It was strange, but with the exception of a few such clear-headed, steadfast "friends of humanity" as Cobden and Bright, and such heroes as those glorious operatives of Lancashire, all seemed changed. Even the sentiments of prominent. Exeter Hall, anti-slavery philanthropists had suffered a secession change, "into something new and strange," especially after the battle of Bull Run—that fortunate calamity for us, as it proved. Most people here were captivated by the splendid qualities of the Confederates—their gallantry, their enthusiasm, their bravery. Before these practical revolutionists, those "moral suasion" agitators, the Northern Abolitionists, made no great show. Garrison with his logic, Burritt with his languages, Douglas with his magnificent eloquence, were as naught to Jefferson Davis and Robert E. Lee, and that soldier of the fine old Cromwellian type—Stonewall Jackson. The "institution" was pronounced in Parliament "not so bad a thing, after all," and the pathetic "Am-I-not-a-Man-and-a-Brother" of Clarkson, became the Sambo of Christie and the "Quashee" of Carlyle. In the midst of this ill-feeling on one side, and sore-feeling on the other, the rash act of a U. S. Naval Officer, in boarding the British steamer *Trent* and seizing the Confederate Envoys, Mason and Slidell, gave England cause, had our Government endorsed that act, for open hostility. So ready, so eager did the English Government seem for a war with America, that it did not wait for an apology, before making extensive military preparations. With that brave but cool-headed Captain on our Ship of State, Abraham Lincoln, and that prudent helmsman, William H. Seward, we could not easily have been driven into a war with England at this time; but we might have been humiliated even more than we were, by the peremptory demands of Lord Palmerston—might have been obliged to eat a piece of "humble pie," so big, hot, and heavy, that it would have remained undigested to this day— had it not been for the prudence, the courtesy, good sense, and admirable tact of the Queen and Prince-Consort in modifying and softening the tone of that important State paper, the demand for an official apology, and the liberation of the Confederate Envoys. It is for this that Americans of the North, and I believe of the South, love Queen Victoria, and not alone for her sake, bless the memory of "Albert the Good."

I know of nothing in literature so exquisite in its pathos and childlike simplicity, as the Queen's own account, in the diary kept faithfully at the time, of the last illness of the Prince-Consort. In it we see the very beatings of her heart, in its hope and fear, love and agony—can mark all the stages of the sacred passion of her sorrow. It is a wonderful psychological study.

That illness in its serious phases, lasted about two weeks. It was a low, slow fever, which at first was not recognized as fever at all, but only a heavy cold. I have been told that the Prince himself had from the first, an impression that he should not recover, and that he talked of his probable death very calmly with his noble daughter Alice, saying: "Your mother cannot bear to hear me speak of it yet." The Queen, though very restless and distressed, and at times shaken with wild alarms, could not face the coming calamity; could not admit the possibility that the sands of that precious life—golden sands, were running out. The alternations of hope and fear, must have been terrible. One morning the Queen records that on going to the Prince she found him looking very wretched: "He did not smile, or take much notice of me. His manner all along was so unlike himself, and he had sometimes, such a strange, wild look." In the evening she writes: "I found my Albert most dear and affectionate and quite himself, when I went in with little Beatrice, whom he kissed. He laughed at some of her new French verses which I made her repeat, then he held her little hand in his for some time, and she stood looking, at him."

For several days he wished to be read to, and the Queen and faithful Alice read his favorite authors; he also asked for music, and Alice played for him some fine German airs. He even wished often to look at a favorite picture, one of Raphael's Madonnas, saying, "It helps me through the day."

At length the fever took on a typhoid form, congestion of the lungs set in, and there was no longer reason for hope,—though they did hope, till almost the last hour. Now, it seems that from the first, even when he did not apparently suffer, except from mortal weariness, there were little fatal indications. One morning he told the Queen that as he lay awake he heard the little birds outside, and "thought of those he used to hear at the Rosenau, in his childhood"; and on the last morning the Queen writes that he "began arranging his hair just as he used to do when well and he was dressing."

It seemed to the poor Queen as though he were "preparing for another and a greater journey" than they had ever taken together. His tenderness towards her through all this sad fortnight, was very touching. It was not calculated to loosen the detaining, clinging clasp of her arms; but it must be very sweet for her to remember. After the weariness of watching, the prostration of fever, he welcomed always the good-morning caress of his "dear little wife." Through the gathering mists of unconsciousness, through the phantom-shades of delirium, his love for her struggled forth, in a tender word, a wistful look, a languid smile, a feeble stroking of the cheek. It was "wondrous pitiful," but it was very beautiful. Even at the last, when he knew no one else, he knew her; and when she bent over him and whispered, "Tis your own little wife," he bowed his head and kissed her.

After she knew that all hope must be given up, the Queen still was able to sit calmly by his bedside, and not trouble with the sound of weeping the peace of that loving, passing soul. Occasionally she felt that she must leave the room and weep, or her suppressed grief would kill her. But she counted the moments and stayed her soul with prayer, to go back to her post.

It was on the night of December 14, 1861, that the beloved Prince-Consort passed away,—quietly and apparently painlessly, from the station he had ennobled, from the home he had blessed. Unconsciously he drifted out on the unknown, mysterious sea, nor knew that loving feet followed him to the strand, and that after him were stretched yearning arms.

That death-bed scene passed in a solemn hush, more mournful than any outcry of passionate grief could be. On one side, knelt the Queen, holding her husband's hand, trying to warm it with kisses and tears; on the other, knelt the Princess Alice. At the foot of the bed, the Prince of Wales and the Princess Helena were kneeling together. It is probable that all the younger children were sleeping in quiet unconsciousness of the presence of the dread angel in the Castle. The Dean of Windsor, Prince Ernest Leiningen,—secretaries, physicians and attached attendants were grouped around. All was silent, save that low, labored breathing, growing softer and softer, and more infrequent, and then—it ceased forever.

I have been told by a lady who had had good opportunities of knowing about the sad circumstances of that death, that the Queen retained perfect possession of herself to the last, and that after the lids had been pressed down over the dear eyes whose light had passed on, she rose calmly, and courteously thanked the physicians in attendance, saying that she knew that everything which human skill and devotion could accomplish, had been done for her husband, whom God had taken. Then she walked out of the death-chamber, erect,—still the Queen, wearing "sorrow's crown of sorrow," and went to her chamber, and shut herself in—her soul alone with God, her heart alone for evermore.

Ah, we may not doubt that this royal being, in whose veins beats the blood of a long, long race of Kings, was brought low enough then,—to her knees, to her face,

"For grief is proud and makes his owner stoop."

91

So absorbing and unwavering had been the love of the Queen for her husband, who to her, was "nobler than the noblest"; such a proud homage of the soul had there been—such a dear habit of the heart, in one with whom habit counted for much, that her people were filled with the most intense anxiety on her behalf. They feared that this cruel stroke which lopped off the best part of her life, would kill her, or plunge her into a depth of melancholy, sadder than death. For some time she was not able to sleep. The thought of that chamber, so lately the scene of all the anxious activity of the sickroom, wherein softly moved troubled physicians and nurses, tearful attendants and awe-struck children, but where now there were shadowed lights, and solemn silence, and where lay that beautiful, marble-like shape, so familiar, yet so strange—that *something* which was not *he*, yet was inexpressibly dear, kept her awake, face to face with her sorrow,—and when at last, the bulletin from Windsor announced, "The Queen has had some hours' sleep," her people all in mourning as they were, felt like ringing joy-bells.

The friend from whom I have before quoted, Mrs. Crosland, a most loyal lady, wrote on this text a very sweet poem, from which I am tempted to give a few verses:

"Sleep, far the night is round thee spread,
Thou daughter of a line of kings;
Sleep, widowed Queen, white angels' wings
Make canopy above thy head!

"Sleep, while a million prayers rise up
To Him who knew all earthly sorrow,
That day by day, each soft to-morrow
May melt the bitter from thy cup.

. . . .

"Long life ask for thee, dear Queen,
And moonlight peace, since joy is set.
And Time's soft touch on dark regret.
And memories calm of what has been!

"Long life for thee—for our best sake.
To be our stay 'mid hopes and fears.
Through many far-off future years,
Till thou by Albert's side shall wake!"

It seems Her Majesty could not bear the thought of her beloved Albert, whose nature was so bright and joyous, and beauty-loving, resting amid the darkness and heavy silence and "cold obstruction" of the royal vault; so, as early as the 18th of December, she drove with the Princess Alice to Frogmore, where they were-received by the Prince of Wales, Prince Louis of Hesse, and several officers of the Royal Household. Then, leaning on the arm of her noble daughter, the Queen walked about the pleasant gardens, till she fixed upon the spot, where now stands the magnificent mausoleum, which, splendid and beautiful as art can make it, is like a costly casket, for the dust, infinitely more precious to her than all the jewels of her crown. It was sweet for her to feel that thus under the shadow of her mother's dear home, the two most sacred loves and sorrows of her life would be forever associated.

There was great and sincere mourning in England among all classes, not alone for the Queen's sake, but for their own, for the Prince-Consort had finally endeared himself to this too long jealous and distrustful people. They had named him "alien," at first; they called him "angel," at last. He was not *that*, but a most rare man, of a nature so sweet and wholesome, of a character so well-balanced and symmetrical, of a life so pure and blameless, that the English cannot reasonably hope to "look upon his like again," not even among his own sons.

92

Some of his contemporaries, while admitting his grace and elegance, were blind to his strength of character, forgetting that a shining column of the Parthenon may be as strong as one of the dark rough-hewn columns of Pæstum. Morally, I believe, the Prince-Consort stands alone in English royal history. What other youth of twenty-one, graceful, beautiful and accomplished, has ever forborne what he forbore?—Ever fought such a good fight against temptations manifold? He was the Sir Galahad of Princes. Being human, he must have been tempted,—if not to a life of sybaritic pleasure, to one of ease, through his delicate organization,—and, through his refined tastes, to one of purely artistic and esthetic culture, which for him, where he was, would have been but splendid selfishness.

Though my estimate of the Prince-Consort is based on his own good words and works, to which I have paid tribute of sincerest praise, it is strengthened and justified by a knowledge of the loving reverence in which his name is held to this day, by the English people of the better class, who honor the Queen for her love stronger than death, and love her the better for it; for I hold,

——"the soul must cast
All weakness from it, all vain strife,
And tread God's ways through this sad life,
To be thus grandly mourned at last."

CHAPTER XXVIII.

The Twilight Life after—Marriage of the Princess Alice—Incidents of the Queen's life at Balmoral—John Brown—A letter from the Queen to the Duchess of Sutherland.

"There is no one near me to call me 'Victoria' now!" is said to have been the desolate cry of the Queen, when, on waking from that first sleep, the cruel morning light, smote upon her with a full consciousness of her bereavement, and a new sense of her royal isolation. She was on a height where the storm beat fiercest and there was the least shelter. Her sacred grief was the business of the world;—she could not long shut herself up with it, and fold her hands in "blameless idleness"; but as the widowed mother and housekeeper in humble life struggles up from the great stroke, and staggers on, resolutely driving back the tears which "hinder needle and thread," and choking down her sobs, to go wearily about her household tasks,—so Victoria, after a little time, rose trembling to her feet, and went through with such imperative State duties as could be delegated to no one. To a near friend, who expressed joy to find her more calm than at the time of her mother's death, she said simply, "I have had God's teaching, and learned to bear all He lays upon me."

There is a record by Lord Beaconsfield of her faithful discharge of such duties a few years later; but what was true of her then, was almost as true an account of the routine of her official life, during a large part of the first years of her widowhood. In a public speech, Beaconsfield said: "There is not a dispatch received from abroad, or sent from this country abroad, which is not submitted to the Queen. The whole of the internal administration of this country greatly depends upon the sign- manual of our Sovereign, and it may be said that her signature has never been placed to any public document of which she did not know the purpose and of which she did not approve. Those cabinet councils of which you all hear, and which are necessarily the scene of anxious and important deliberation, are reported, on their termination, by the Minister to the Sovereign, and they often call from her critical remarks requiring considerable attention; and I will venture to say that no person likely to administer the affairs of this country would be likely to treat the suggestions of Her Majesty with indifference, for at this moment there is probably no person living who has such complete control over the political condition of England as the Sovereign herself."

I have come upon few incidents of that first sad year. The Princess Alice was married very quietly at Osborne, and went away to her German home, where she lived for seventeen happy years, a noble and beneficent life. In character she was very like her father—to whose soul hers was so knit, that, when in her last illness, the anniversary of his death came round, she seemed to hear his call, and went to him at once in child- like obedience. She took that fatal illness—the diphtheria—from a dear child in a kiss, "the kiss of death," as Lord Beaconsfield called it.

The Rev. Norman McLeod has left a record of the widowed Queen's first visit to Balmoral. It seems he thought she was too unreconciled to her loss, and felt it his duty to preach what he believed to be "truth in God's sight, and that which I believe she needed," he said, "though I felt it would be very trying for her to receive it." She did receive it very sweetly, and wrote him "a kind, tender letter of thanks for it," She afterwards summoned him to the castle, and to her own room. He writes: "She was alone. She met me with an unutterably sad expression, which filled my eyes with tears, and at once began to speak about the Prince. ... She spoke of his excellencies—his love, his cheerfulness; how he was everything to her. She said she never shut her eyes to trials, but liked to look them in the face; how she would never shrink from duty, but that all was at present done mechanically; that her highest ideas of purity and love were obtained from him, and that God could not be displeased with her love."

No, we cannot love enough to displease the God of love, who is not, whatever men may preach, a "jealous God," in that small way; but perhaps we may grieve too much to please the Master of Life, of which, in His eyes, what we call death, is the immortal blossom and crowning.

It seems to me that in her loving tribute to the Prince, the Queen was a little unjust to her mother, to whose precepts and example she owed very high "ideas of purity" and that strong sense of duty, and that fortitude, essentially a womanly, not a manly, virtue, which preserved her through the temptations of a glad and splendid youth—through the trials and sorrows of maturer years, and which, when that time of bitterest trial came, braced up her shattered forces, and held together her broken heart.

Balmoral—the dear mountain-home, so entirely her husband's creation—now became more than ever dear to the Queen, and has never lost its charm for her. Her life there has been, from the first, almost pastoral in its simplicity.

The Highlanders about them, a primitive, but very proud people, regarded their Sovereign and her husband with no servile awe. With them, even respect begins, like charity, at home; what there is left, they give loyally to their superiors in rank. To the Queen and her family they have given more,—love and free-hearted devotion. Her Majesty has always gone about among the poorer tenants of the estate, like any laird's wife, in an unpretending, neighborly way; and they, thanks to their good Scotch sense and Highland pride, never take advantage of the uncondescending condescension, to offend her by too great familiarity, or shock her by servility. Taking up her "Journal," I have chanced upon an account given by Her Majesty of a round of visits to the cottages of certain "poor old women," and here is an entry or two:

"Before we went into any, we met a woman who was very poor, and eighty- eight years old. I gave her a warm petticoat, and the tears rolled down her old cheeks, and she shook my hands and prayed God to bless me: it was very touching.

"I went into a small cabin of old Kitty Kear's, who is eighty-six years old, quite-erect, and who welcomed us with a great air of dignity. She sat down and spun. I gave her, also, a warm petticoat. She said, 'May the Lord ever attend ye and yours, here and hereafter; and may the Lord be a guide to ye, and keep ye fra all harm.'"

Now, some readers, whose ideas of royal charities are derived from the kings and queens of melodrama, who fling about golden largess, or "chuck" plethoric purses at their poor subjects, may be amused at these entries in a great Queen's journal, but "let them laugh who win"—the flannel petticoats.

During a later visit to the widowed Queen at Balmoral, Dr. McLeod writes: "After dinner, the Queen invited me to her room, where I found the Princess Helena and the Marchioness of Ely. The Queen sat down to spin on a fine Scotch wheel, while I read Burns to her—'*Tam O'Shanter*,' and '*A Man's a Man for a' That*'—her favorites."

In the Queen's book I find frequent pleasant mention of the young Highlander, John Brown—a favorite personal attendant, first of Prince Albert, and afterwards of Her Majesty.

She had the misfortune to lose this "good and faithful servant," in the early part of this year. In a foot-note in her "Journal," she paid a grateful tribute to his "attention, care and faithfulness"—to his rare devotion to her, especially during a period of physical weakness and nervous prostration, when such service as his was invaluable. She also says of him, "He has all the independence and elevation of feeling peculiar to the Highland race, and is singularly straightforward, simple- minded, kind-hearted and disinterested."

If there is something touching in the nearly life-long service and devotion of the Highlander, almost always seen so close behind his Liege Lady, when she appeared in public, that he was named "the Queen's shadow"—there is something admirable in her grateful appreciation of that service, in her frank acknowledgment of all she has owed of comfort, in a constant sense of security, to this man's steadfast faithfulness; and now that the "shadow" has gone before, I hold it is only fitting and loyal in her to acknowledge for him, as she does, "friendship," and even "affection"—not only to lay flowers on his grave, but to pay more enduring tribute to his honest memory. He was a Highland gillie, of simple Highland ways and words but "*A man's a man for a' that.*" If Byron could nurse his dying dog, *Boatswain*, and erect a monument to his memory, and not lose, but gain, our respect by so doing, we surely might let pass, unquestioned, the Queen's grief for a faithful human creature— for thirty-four years devoted to her—ever at her call—looking up to her, yet watching over her; a friend, whose humble good sense and canny bits of counsel must often, in the simpler, yet not simple, affairs of her complex life, be sorely missed.

That is how it strikes an American, of democratic tendencies.

About a year after the death of Prince Albert, the Duchess of Sutherland presented to the Queen a richly-bound Bible, the offering of loyal "English widows."

In her letter of acknowledgment, Her Majesty gives very strong and clear expression to her faith, not only in the happy continued existence of her beloved husband, but in his "unseen presence" with her—a faith which she has often expressed. The letter runs thus:

"MY DEAREST DUCHESS:—I am deeply touched by the gift of a Bible 'from many widows,' and by the very kind and affectionate address which accompanied it. ... Pray express to all these kind sister-widows the deep and heartfelt gratitude of their widowed Queen, who can never feel grateful enough for the universal sympathy she has received, and continues to receive, from her loyal and devoted subjects. But what she values far more is their appreciation of her adored and perfect husband. To her, the only sort of consolation she experiences is in the constant sense of his unseen presence and the blessed thought of the Eternal Union hereafter, which will make the bitter anguish of the present appear as naught. That our Heavenly Father may impart to 'many widows' those sources of consolation and support, is their broken-hearted Queen's earnest prayer ... Believe me ever yours most affectionately, VICTORIA."

Dean Stanley is reported as telling of a touching little circumstance which he received from the Princess Hohenlohe (Feodore), from which it seems that Her Majesty was for a long time in the habit of going every morning to look at the cows on Prince Albert's model farm, because "*he* had been used to do so," feeling, perhaps, that the gentle creatures might miss him—that somewhere in their big dull brains, they might wonder where their friend could be, and why he did not come. The Princess also said that her poor sister found her only comfort in the belief that her husband's spirit was close beside her—for he had promised her that it should be so.

CHAPTER XXIX.

Arrival in England of the Princess Alexandra to wed the Prince of Wales— Garibaldi's visit to London—The Queen's first public appearance after her widowhood—Marriage of the Princess Louise—Illness of the Prince of Wales—Disaffection in Ireland—The Queen's sympathy during the illness of President Garfield.

On the 7th of March, 1863, all London and nearly all England went mad over the coming of the Princess Alexandra, from Denmark, to wed the Prince of Wales. Lord Ronald Gower, a son of the beautiful Duchess of Sutherland, gives in his "Reminiscences" a fine description of her arrival in London, and of the wedding at Windsor three days after. He says: "Probably since the day in Paris when Marie Antoinette was acclaimed in the gardens of the Tuileries, no Princess ever had so enthusiastic a reception, or so quickly won the hearts of thousands by the mere charm of her presence." This writer gives a very vivid description of the crowd which waited patiently for hours, of a cold, wretched day, for the sight of that sweet face whose sweetness has never yet cloyed upon them. At last, there came a small company of Life Guards, escorting an open carriage-and-four, containing the young Danish Princess and His Royal Highness Albert Edward, looking very happy and very conscious. The smiling, blushing, appealing face of the Princess warmed as well as won all hearts. There were few flowers at that season to scatter on her way, except flowers of poetry, of which there was no jack. Tennyson's pretty ode has not been forgotten, but all as noble and sweet was the greeting of her from whom I have before quoted; Mrs. Crosland. The most touching, though not the strongest verse in that poem, is this:

"She comes another child to be
To that Crowned Widow of the land,
Whose sceptre weighs more heavily
Since One has ceased to hold her hand."

The Queen did not feel herself equal to taking any part in the marriage ceremony, but looked down upon the scene of grandeur and gayety from the Royal Gallery of St George's Chapel. The Duchess of Sutherland attended her then for the last time. She had been with her at her coronation and marriage; to-day they were both widows, and must have been at the moment living intensely and sorrowfully in the past. With the exception of the Crown Princess of Germany and the Duke of Edinburgh, all the Queen's children, down to little Beatrice, were present. The bride, it is stated, "looked lovely; she did not raise her eyes once in going into, and but little in going out of, the Chapel on her husband's arm."

This first daughter-in-law soon made a place for herself in the Queen's heart, by her grace and amiability. I have heard a pretty little story of an attempt of hers to lighten somewhat Her Majesty's heavy cloud of mourning. Millinery being one of her accomplishments, she prevailed upon the Queen to let her remodel her bonnet, which she did, principally by removing a small basketful of sombre weeds. The Queen saw through her little *ruse* and shook her head mournfully,—but wore the bonnet.

The next year London went still more mad over Garibaldi. His enthusiastic admirers almost mobbed Stafford House, at which he was entertained by the young Duke of Sutherland Lord Ronald Gower describes that memorable visit and the popular excitement very vividly.

The Italian hero entered that beautiful palace, where a grand company of the nobility were waiting to receive him, attired in a rough gray overcoat and trousers, a large pork-pie hat, a loose black neck-tie, and a red flannel shirt. This he never changed—I mean his style of dress, not the shirt—but Garibaldi would have been quite un-Garibaldi-ed in an English evening suit. Lord Ronald Gower writes that his noble, liberty- loving mother was very devoted to their guest, but does not add that by so doing she shocked the sensibilities of footmen and housemaids. One of the latter once told to another guest, a moving story of the strange habits of "Italian brigand": "Why, marm," she said, "he was such a common-looking person, and he would get up so awful early and go hobbling about in the garden. One morning at six o'clock, I looked out of my window, and there he was walking up and down, and the Duchess with him— *my* Duchess, walking and talking with the likes of him!"

The first public appearance of the widowed Queen was at the opening of Parliament, in 1866. I do not know whether the splendid chair of State she had provided for Prince Albert, in the happy old time, had been left in its place, to smite her eyes with its gilding and her heart with its emptiness; I do not know whether its presence or its absence would have grieved her most; but every sorrowing widow knows what it is to look on her husband's vacant chair. It does not matter whether it is made of rude, unpainted wood and woven rushes, or is a golden and velvet- cushioned chair of State,—it was *his* seat, and he is gone! Queen Victoria must have felt that day, in her lonely grandeur, like crying out with Constance,

"Here I and Sorrow sit. "

Lady Bloomfield gives a very touching account of her first visit to the widowed mistress, whom, nearly twenty years before, she had so gladly and proudly served—for true service is in the spirit, though the act may be limited to taking a part in a duet, or handing the daily bouquet. She wrote: "The Queen is dreadfully changed—most sad, but with the gentlest, most benevolent smile. Even when the tears rolled down her cheeks, she tried to smile." I think it was about this time that the Queen presented to our George Peabody her portrait, expressly painted for him, in recognition of his more than princely munificence in the gift of model lodging-houses to the London poor. It was a small portrait—enameled, I believe. I do not think it was an idealized picture, though the pencil was evidently guided by a delicate and reverential loyalty, "doing its spiriting gently," in marking the tracings of time and sorrow. In a description which I wrote at the tune of its exhibition in Philadelphia, I said: "With the exception of a touching expression of habitual sadness, this face is very like the one I looked down upon from the gallery of the House of Lords fifteen years ago. There is the same roundness of outline, only 'a little more so'—almost the same freshness of tints in the fair complexion. The soft brown hair is unchanged in color, if somewhat thinner; and the clear blue eyes have the same steady outlook. The whole figure is marked by a sort of regal rigidity. The face, if not positively unhappy in expression, is quite empty of happiness. There is about it an atmosphere of lonely state and absolute widowhood. The Mary Stuart cap is very becoming to Her Majesty, but the black dress mars the picturesque effect of the portrait. The neck and arms have all the roundness of youth, and are exquisitely painted. I remember hearing the late Mr. Gibson, who made several statues of the Queen, say that loyalty itself need not to flatter her arms or bust; in sculpture or painting, as they were really remarkably beautiful."

In 1868 the Queen had the misfortune to lose her "dearest Duchess"—that grandest daughter of the grand house of Howard, *the* Duchess of Sutherland. She floated all unconsciously out on the waves that wash against the restful palm-crowned shore, her last words being, "I think I shall sleep now—I am so tired."

The Princess Louise was married with really royal pomp and a brave attempt at the old gayety, in St. George's Chapel, Windsor, in March, 1871, to the Marquis of Lome.

The bride, who, according to Lord Ronald Gower, was. "very pale, but handsome as she always is," was accompanied by the Prince of Wales; her uncle, the Grand Duke of Coburg; and, to the great joy of all the assembly, by her mother, the Queen. The wedded pair went to Claremont for their honeymoon. As they drove away, "rice and white satin slippers were sent after them, and John Brown threw a new broom, Highland fashion."

The people were much comforted at this appearance of the Queen once more in the great gay world. They had begun to think that her social seclusion would never end. When she went down into the "valley of the shadow of death" with her beloved, though she struggled bravely up alone, she brought the shadow with her; it enveloped her and wrapped her away from her subjects—even the most loving and sympathetic. Now they took heart, believing that royalty was finally coming out from under its eclipse of mourning, that the Court would be re-established in Buckingham Palace, and things generally, go on as in the good old days. They never did, however, and never will, under her reign. It is too much to ask of her, it seems.

Whether it is true, as I hear, that the air of London is hurtful to her, giving her severe headaches, or that the scenes of her childhood and early queenhood, and of her marriage, are too much for her, and heart- ache is the matter, I know not; but it is undeniable that the Queen prefers any one of her other homes to Buckingham Palace. She only comes to it when absolute compelled by the duties of State. It is hard for London tradesmen and pleasure-seekers, who think Her Majesty's mourning immoderate, and doubt whether their wives would fret so long for them; but when, in the first year of her, reign, the pretty, wilful Victoria said to Lord Melbourne: "What is the use of being a Queen if one cannot do as one likes!" her people laughed and applauded. Surely, with years and trouble, and much faithful care and labor, and has not lost the right to have a mind of her own, or the will to maintain it.

Of late years I have seen Her Majesty some half dozen times; once on her way to prorogue Parliament, seated in the grand State coach, drawn by the superb, cream-colored State horses, in all imaginable splendor of trappings—escorted by the dashing Life Guards, and all the royal carriages, each with its resplendent coachman and footmen, most gorgeous of human creatures, and inside, very nice and respectable-looking people, with no particular air of pride or elation. The Queen wore a cloak of ermine, a tiara of diamonds, and a long, cloud-like veil of tulle, floating back from her face, which that day had a very pleasant, genial expression. She is changed,—of course she is; but she has even more of the old calm dignity, and when she smiles, the effect is magical; her youth flashes over her face, and quite the old look—the look *he* knew her by, comes back for a little while.

At other times I have had glimpses of her as her carriage dashed through the gateway to Marlborough House, on a garden-party day, or through the Park, as she was fleeing with all speed from the city, after a Drawing- room. Sometimes, she has bowed right and left, and smiled, as though pleased by the cheers of the people; but at other times she has scarcely inclined her head, and worn a look of unsmiling, utter weariness—proving that a woman may have much worldly goods, many jewels, and brave velvet gowns, and heaps of India shawls, and half a dozen grand mansions, with a throne in every one, and yet at times feel that this brief life of ours is "all vanity and vexation of spirit."

The Queen, though she had not kept up her intimate relations with the Emperor and Empress, was shocked at the utter ruin to them and their son, which resulted from the French and Prussian war, and she was not wanting in tender sympathy, when the poor frightened refugee, Eugenie, hid a tearful face against her sisterly breast, and sobbed out, "I have been too favorable to war." To the Emperor she granted an asylum and a grave.

I know not whether France will ever demand his dust, to give it sepulture under the dome of the Invalides; but he has already on the banks of the Seine the grandest of monuments—*Paris*. His memory stands fair and firm in stately buildings and massive bridges, and is renewed every year in the plane tree of noble Boulevards, those green *longas vias*, grander than the military highways of the Caesars.

In 1867 the Prince of Wales fell grievously ill, with the same fearful malady that had deprived him of his father. Intense was the anxiety not only of the Royal Family, but of all the English people the world over. Soon the sympathy of other nations was aroused, and prayers began to ascend to Heaven for the preservation of that precious life, not only from all Christian peoples, but from Hebrews, Mohammedans and Buddhists; in heathen lands the missionaries prayed, and in heathen portions of Christian cities the mission-children prayed, while on the high seas the sailors responded fervently when the captain. read in the Service the "Prayer for the Sick," meaning their Prince, "sick unto death." The fine old boast of England's power, that "her morning drum beats round the world," how poor it seems beside the thought, of this zone of prayer! There had been nothing like this in English history, and there was nothing like it in ours, till that heart-breaking time of the mortal illness of President Garfield. O, worthy should be, the life and manifold the good works of that man for whom so many peoples and tongues have given surety to Heaven by fervent intercessions and supplications.

This long sad time of anxiety and peril drew the Queen out of her sorrow as nothing had done before. She watched tenderly by the bedside of her son, and when he was recovered, and went to St. Paul's to return thanks, she sat by his side, and wore a white flower in her bonnet, and her grateful smile showed that there was a rift in the cloud of her mourning, and that God's sunlight was striking through.

Lord Ronald Gower quotes a letter from his sister, the Duchess of Westminster, describing the Prince and Princess of Wales as she saw them about this time. She said: "He is much thinner and his head shaved, but little changed in his face, and looking so grateful. She looks thin and worn, but so affectionate—tears in her eyes when talking of him, and his manner to her so gentle."

Surely convalescence is a "state of grace." Would that it might always last a lifetime with us!

During this year, Irish disaffection broke out very seriously in the great Fenian movement. An upheaval this, from the lowest stratum of society, with no gentlemen, or eloquent orators, for leaders, but all the more appalling for that. These rough, desperate men meant, as they said, "business." This movement <was suppressed, driven under the surface, but only to break out more appallingly than ever some ten or twelve years later, in brutal assassinations, which have curdled the blood of the world. Ah, must it always be so? Will this tiresome old Celtic Enceladus never lie quiet, and be dead, though the mountain sit upon him ever so solidly, and smoke ever so placidly above him?

Where now, we sadly ask, is the Ireland of Tom Moore, Father Prout, Lover and Lever? Not enough left of it to furnish a new drama for Mr. Boucicault. Donnybrook Fair has given place to midnight conspirations. Fox-hunts to the stalking of landlords—all the jolly old customs extinct, except the "wake." Peasant-life, over there, sometimes seems, at the best, one protracted "wake."

I suppose it is too late now, yet I can but think that if the Queen had built years ago, a palace in Ireland, at Killarney, or in lovely Wicklow, or in Dublin itself, and resided there a part of every year, things might have been better. She was so popular in that "distressful country" when, by frequent visits, she testified an interest in it, and her gentle, motherly presence might have had a more placating influence than any "Coercion bill." The money she would have spent there,—the very crumbs that would have fallen from her table, would have been a benefaction to that poor people.

The Fenian drama had its ghastly closing *tableau* in the hanging of the ringleaders, and the explosion at Clerkenwell. The hanging of those Fenians must have been about the last of that sort of a public entertainment, as a law was soon passed making all future executions strictly private. Among a certain class of Her Majesty's subjects this was a most unpopular measure. Pot-house politicians and gin-palace courtiers, both ladies and gentlemen, discussed it hotly and denounced it sternly, as an infringement on the sacred immemorial rights of British freemen and a blow to the British Constitution.

In 1874 Mr. Disraeli had become Prime Minister. He died in 1880—Lord Beaconsfield, sincerely lamented by the Queen, who was much attached to him as a friend, and greatly admired him as a man of genius. He was a brilliant novelist and a famous statesman; but the best things I know of him are the tender love and manly gratitude he always testified towards his devoted wife, and his pathetic mourning for her loss. He might have adopted for her tombstone the quaint, terse epitaph of an American husband—"Think what a wife should be, and she was that."

Through his means, the title of "Empress of India" was conferred on the Queen by act of Parliament. Some English people opposed it as superfluous, a sort of anti-climax of dignity, as "gilding the refined gold" of English Sovereignty with baser metal, as "painting the lily" of the noblest of English royal titles with India-ink; but it did no harm. It did not hurt the Radicals and it pleased the Rajahs.

Then came the Zulu war, with its awful disasters in the inglorious slaughter of some thousands of gallant young soldiers, among which, because of the power of romantic, historic associations, the death of the young Prince Imperial stands out in woful relief. This was a severe personal shock to the Queen. With all her tender sympathy she tried to console the inconsolable Empress, and with her sons paid funeral honors to the memory of the Prince, who had been almost as one of her family. The only time I ever saw him he was in their company, driving away from a royal garden-party.

The Prince of Wales visited India, traveled and hunted extensively, was fêted after the most gorgeous Oriental style, and brought home rich presents enough to set up a grand Eastern bazaar in Marlborough House, and animals enough to start a respectable menagerie. Everywhere he went he inclined the hearts of the people to peace and loyalty, by his frank and genial ways. Does His Royal Highness ever propose such a tour in Ireland? He would not probably receive as tribute so much jewelry and gorgeous merchandise—so many tigers, pythons and other little things; but there is a fine chance for giving over there, and we read: "It is more blessed to give, than to receive."

I come now to that period of our national history with which the Queen of England so kindly, so "gently and humanly" associated herself—I mean the illness and death of President Garfield. To this day, that association is a drop of sweetness in the bitter cup of our sorrow and humiliation. From the 2d of July, 1881, the date of her first telegram of anxious inquiry addressed to our Minister, to the 27th of the following September, when she telegraphed her tender solicitude as to the condition of "the late President's mother," not a week went by that she did not send to Mr. Lowell sympathetic messages, asking for the latest news—congratulating or condoling, as the state of "the world's patient" fluctuated between life and death—and when all was over, she at once telegraphed directly to Mrs. Garfield in these words of tenderest commiseration, so worthy of her great heart:

"Words cannot express the deep sympathy I feel with you at this terrible moment. May God support and comfort you as He alone can."

She afterwards sent an autograph letter to Mrs. Garfield, and also asked for a photograph of the President.

No American who was in London at that time, especially on the day of or President's funeral, so universally observed throughout Great Britain, can ever forget the generous, whole-souled sympathy of the English people, in part at least, inspired by the words 'and acts of the English Queen. The intense interest with which she had watched that melancholy struggle between "the Two Angels," over that distant death-bed, and the grief with which she beheld the issue were known and responded to, and so the noble contagion spread. It was not needed, perhaps, that signs of mourning should be shown in her Palace windows, to have them appear as they did, all over the vast city, but it was something strange and affecting to see those blinds of a proud royal abode lowered out of respect for the memory of a republican ruler, and sympathy for an untitled "sister-widow."

We respected all those signs of mourning about us then—were grateful for them all, from the flag at half-mast and the tolling bell, to the closing of the shop of the small tradesman, and the bit of crape on the whip of the cabman.

CHAPTER XXX.

My reasons for Honoring the Queen—Anecdotes—Some democratic reflections upon the Queen's position and her Subjects' loyalty—The Royal Children— Last words.

My reasons for admiring and honoring Queen Victoria are, perhaps, amply revealed in this little book, but I will briefly recapitulate them: First, is her great power of loving, and tenacity in holding on to love. Next is her loyalty—that quality which makes her stand steadfastly by those she loves, through good and evil report, arid not afraid to do honor to a dead friend, be he prince or peasant—that quality which in her lofty position, makes her friendship for the unfortunate exile "as the shadow of a great rock in a weary land."

Next I place her sincerity, her downright honesty, which makes falsehood and duplicity in those she has to do with, something to be wondered over as well as scorned. Next, is her courage, so abundantly shown in the many instances in which her life has been menaced. I do not believe that a braver woman lives than Queen Victoria.

I admire her also for the respect and delicate consideration which she has always had for the royalty of intellect, for the pride and sensitiveness of genius. This peculiarity dates far back to when, as the young Princess Victoria, she timidly asked that such men as the poets Moore and Rogers, and the actors Charles Kemble and Macready might be presented to her. Thomas Campbell used to relate an incident showing what charming compliments she knew how to pay to poets. Wishing to witness the coronation, he wrote to the Earl Marshal, saying: "There is a place in the Abbey called 'The Poets' Corner,' which suggests the possibility of there being room in it for living poets also." This brought him a ticket of admission. His admiration of the young Queen's behavior was unbounded, and he says: "On returning home, I resolved out of pure esteem and veneration, to send her a copy of all say works. Accordingly I had them, bound up and went personally with them to Sir Henry Wheatley, who, when he understood my errand, told me that Her Majesty made it a rule to decline presents of this kind, as it placed her under obligations which were not pleasant to her. 'Say to Her Majesty, Sir Henry,' I replied, 'that there is nothing which the Queen can touch with her sceptre in any of her dominions which I covet; and I therefore entreat you to present them with my devotion as a subject.' But the next day they were returned. I hesitated to open the parcel, but on doing so I found to my inexpressible joy a note enclosed, desiring my autograph on them. Having complied with this wish, I again transmitted the books to Her Majesty, and in the course of a day or two, received in return this elegant portrait engraving, with Her Majesty's autograph, as you see, below."

The Queen was the friend of Charles Kingsley, and of Charles Dickens, in his later days. In presenting the latter with her. book, "*Leaves from a Journal of Our Life in the Highlands*" she spoke of herself as "the humblest of writers," and as almost ashamed to offer it, even with her priceless autograph, to "one of the greatest." Mr. Tennyson she delights to honor with her friendship. I have read a little story of her calling on him at his place, on the Isle of Wight. It seems he had not received due notice, or that, absorbed in writing, he had forgotten the hour. At all events, he was taken by surprise, and was obliged to run out to receive Her Majesty in his dressing-gown and slippers, and with his hair disheveled, as it had become in the fine frenzy of composition. Just think of Mr. Tennyson with his hair more than usually disheveled! Of course it was all right, as far as the Queen was concerned,—but then the footmen!

In her youth, the Queen was very fond of the drama, and did honor to its representations, as we have seen. Rachel used to show, with especial pride, a costly bracelet, within which was the inscription, "*Victoria à Rachel*." When the beautiful English actress, Mrs. Warner, was slowly dying of cancer, the Queen, I am told, used to send daily one of her carriages to take her out for a drive—as the actress could not afford herself such a luxury.

Of Americans distinguished for talent, Her Majesty has never failed to show, when in her power, a generous appreciation. As long ago as 1839, she invited to Buckingham Palace, Daniel Webster and Mrs. Webster. To our great statesman—who Miss Mitford, at the time, said was "the grandest- looking man" she had ever beheld, and whom Sydney Smith called, more tersely than elegantly, "a steam-engine in breeches"—the Queen was especially attentive, talking much with him; and he pronounced her "very intelligent." To Longfellow, purest of poets and sweetest of spirits, she showed a respect which was almost homage; and I am told that in Mr. Lowell, she respects the poet and the scholar, even more than the Minister. Ah, he is one whose poetic genius, whose scholarship, keen wit, and, above all, exquisite humor, the Prince-Consort would have appreciated and delighted in.

Artists and men of letters have never been behindhand in tributes to the Queen. Every sculptor and painter to whom she has sat, has had the same story as Gibson and Leslie to tell of her kindness, taste and intelligence. Miss Fox, writing of Landseer, says, "He deeply admires the Queen's intellect, which he thinks superior to any woman's in Europe. Her memory is so remarkable that he has known her recall exact words of speeches, made years ago, which the speakers themselves had forgotten."

That was saying too much, I think, when Mrs. Somerville, Miss Martineau, and Elizabeth Barrett were living, and working, in England. In the things pertaining to her station and vocation, Victoria doubtless was, and is, superior to any woman in Europe. The Duke of Wellington, who thought at fink that he could not get on with her, because he had "no small talk," finally enjoyed conversing with her on the most serious matters of State. Sir Archibald Alison, in describing an evening with her and Prince Albert, says: "The Queen took her full share in the conversation, and I could easily see, from her quickness of apprehension. And the questions she put to those around her, that she possessed uncommon talent, a great desire for information, and, in particular, great rapidity of thought—a faculty often possessed by persons of her rank, and arising not merely from natural ability, but from the habit of conversing with the first men of the age."

Ah, I wonder if Her Majesty has ever realized her blessed privilege in being able to converse freely with "the first men of the age"; to avow her interest in politics, which is history flowing by; in statesmanship, that cunning tapestry-work of empire, without fearing to be set down as "a strong-minded female out of her sphere."

Much has been told me of the Queen's shrewdness and perspicacity. An English gentleman, who has opportunities of knowing much of her, lately said to me: "Her Majesty has an eagle-eye; she sees everything—sees everybody—sees through everybody." And this reminded me of a little anecdote, told me many years before, by an English fellow-traveler,—the story of a little informal interview, which amusingly revealed not only the Queen's quickness of perception, but directness of character.

My informant was a young gentleman of very artistic tastes—a passionate picture-lover. He had seen all the great paintings in the public galleries of London, and had a strong desire to see those of Buckingham Palace, which, that not being a show-house, are inaccessible to an ordinary connoisseur. Fortune favored him at <last. He was the brother of a London carpet merchant, who had an order to put down new carpets in the State apartments of the palace; and so it chanced that the temptation came to my friend to put on a workman's blouse and thus enter the royal precincts, while the flag, indicating the presence of the august family, floated defiantly over the roof. So he effected an entrance, and, when once within the royal halls, dropped his assumed character and devoted himself to the pictures. It happened that he remained in one of the apartments after the workmen had left, and, while quite alone, the Queen came tripping in, wearing a plain white morning-dress, and followed by two or three of her younger children, dressed with like simplicity. She approached the supposed workman and, said: "Pray can you tell me when the new carpet will be put down in the Privy Council Chamber?" and he, thinking he had no right to appear to recognize the Queen under the circumstances, replied: "Really, madam—I cannot tell—but I will enquire." "Stay," she said abruptly, but not unkindly; "who are you? I perceive that you are not one of the workmen." Mr. W——, blushing and stammering somewhat, yet made a clean breast of it, and told the simple truth. The Queen seemed much amused with his *ruse*, and, for the sake of his love for art, forgave it; then added, smiling, "I knew, for all your dress, that you were a gentleman, because you did not address me as 'your Majesty.' Pray look at the pictures as long as you will. Good-morning! Come, chicks, we must go."

I hear that a distinguished American friend has expressed a fear that I shall "idealize Queen Victoria." I do not think I have done so. I leave that to her English biographers and eulogists. In my researches, I have come upon curious things, in the way of pompous panegyric, which would have made Minerva the Wise, feel foolish, and which Juno the Superb, would have pronounced "a little too strong, really." I have not, it is true, pointed out faults—I have not been near enough to "the Queen's Most Excellent Majesty" to become acquainted with them. I presume she has them—I hope she has. I think all writers who deny her human weaknesses, or betray surprise at any exhibition of ordinary human feeling, pay the Queen a very poor compliment. There is in England a good deal of exaggerated expression of loyalty. Such words as "gracious" and "condescending" are habits and forms of speech. Of the real sentiment of loyalty, I do not think there is an excess—at least not toward the Queen. When Her Majesty gives way to natural emotion over the death of a friend, or over a great public calamity, I do not believe she likes to have the fact made a circumstance of. For instance, when that dreadful tragedy occurred in the Victoria Hall, at Sunderland, when hundreds of children perished, by being trampled underfoot and suffocated, the Court intelligence, which seemed to deepen the sadness in many minds, was that "Her Majesty was observed to weep on reading the account." This item went the rounds, and called forth such expressions of sympathy that one would have supposed that it was the august *mater patriæ* at Windsor, who had been bereaved, and not those poor distracted mothers at Sunderland. Why should the Queen not weep over such a "massacre of the innocents," like any other good, sympathetic, motherly woman? She has not wept away all her tears for herself.

I remember at the time of the death of Lady Augusta Stanley, who had formerly been one of Her Majesty's Maids of Honor, much was said of the Queen's sympathy with the Dean. She attended the funeral, and afterwards, it is said, "led the widowed mourner into his desolate home." This act, so simple and sweet in a friend, was, I know, looked upon' by some as "condescension," in a sovereign; but how could one sorrowing human soul condescend to another—and that other Arthur Stanley? Sorrow is as great a leveler as death. Tears wash away all poor human distinctions.

We also took the Queen's sympathy with us, in our great national- bereavement, too much as though it were something quite super-royal, if not superhuman. It was the exquisite wording of those telegrams which touched, melted our hearts; but we should have been neither surprised, nor overcome. It was beautiful, but it was natural. *She* could not have said less, or said it differently. It was very sweet of her to send that floral offering, known and dear to us all as "the Queen's Wreath," but she sacrificed no dignity in so doing, as her flowers were to lie on the coffin of the ruler of a great empire—a ruler who had been as much greater than an ordinary monarch as election is greater than accident.

Of course, as the Queen is the most interesting personage in all England, the least little things connected with her have an interest which Americans can hardly understand. In a handsome semi-official work called "A Diary of Royal Events," I find gravely related the story of an Osborne postman, who once lent the Queen and Prince Albert his umbrella, and was told to call for it at the great house, when he received it back, and with it a five-pound note. I see nothing very note-worthy in this, except the fact, honorable to humanity, of a borrowed umbrella being promptly returned, the owner calling for it. The five-pound note, though, was an "event" to the postman.

A few concluding words about the Queen's children, who with many grandchildren "rise up to call her blessed."

Victoria, the Crown Princess of Germany, is a fine-looking woman, with the same peculiarly German face, "round as an apple," which she had as a child. She is very clever, especially in art, and her character, formed under her father's hand, very noble. The Prince of Wales is a hard- working man in his way, which means in many ways, for the public benefit- -industrial, artistic, scientific and social. The people seem bent on making him true to his old Saxon motto—"*Ich dien*" (I serve). He is exceedingly popular, being very genial and affable—not jealous, it is said, of his dignity as a Prince, but very jealous of his dignity as a gentleman—and that is right; for kings may come, and kings may go, but the fine type of the English gentleman goes on forever. No revolution can depose it; no commune can destroy it—it is proof against dynamite.

A handsome man is the Duke of Edinburgh (Prince Alfred), who no longer follows the sea, but is settled down in England, with his wife, a daughter of the late Czar, who testified by this alliance his wish to let Crimean "by-gones be by-gones"—till the next time, at least.

The Duke resembles his father in his love for and cultivation of music. There does not seem to be any opening for him to play a part like that of Alfred the Great, but he can probably play the violin better than that monarch ever did. They drew another sort of a bow in those old days.

The Princess Christian of Schleswig-Holstein (Princess Helena) is in appearance most like her mother, and perhaps in character and tastes, as she lives a life of quiet retirement, is a devoted wife and-mother, yet often giving her time and energies to a good work, or an artistic enterprise. She also is exceedingly fond of music and is an accomplished pianist. A passion for music belongs to this family by a double inheritance. Even poor, old, blind George the Third consoled himself at his organ, for the loss of an empire and the darkening of as world.

The Duke of Connaught, whom we so pleasantly remember in America as Prince Arthur, is the soldier of the family—a real one, since he won his spars in Egypt. He has something of the grave, gentle look of his father, and is much liked and respected.

The Princess Louise (Marchioness of Lorne) is a beautiful woman, but with a somewhat cold and proud expression, a veritable *grande dame*. She is remarkably clever and accomplished, especially in art—modeling admirably well—for a Princess.

Prince Leopold (Duke of Albany) is the scholar of the family— intellectually and morally more like Prince Albert, it is said, than any of his brothers. I was once told by the eminent Dr. James Martineau, who had met and conversed with him, that he was a young man of a very thoughtful mind, high aims, and quite remarkable acquirements. As Dr. Martineau is not of *the* church, being a Unitarian divine, he cannot be suspected, in pronouncing such eulogies on the Queen's darling son, of having an eye to preferment-of working for a "living." On the whole, Her Majesty's sons are a decided improvement on her six royal uncles, on the paternal side.

We come now to the youngest, the darling and delight of her father, the little one who "stood and looked at him," when he lay ill, marveling at the mysterious change in his dear face;—the Princess Beatrice—as closely associated, as constantly with her mother as was the Princess Victoria with the Duchess of Kent. She also is accomplished and clever, nor appears in any way to "unbeseem the promise of her spring." She also has the love of music which marks her race. She was little more than a baby when her father went away, and her innocent wonder and questioning must often have pierced her mother's wounded heart anew; and yet those little loving hands must have helped to draw that mother from the depths of gloom and despair in which she was so nearly engulfed. Though the youngest of all, her father seems to have delegated to her much of his dearest earthly care, and she the good daughter, is, it may be, led by unseen hands, and inspired by unspoken words of counsel and acceptance. So, though the life of the Princess Beatrice is not abounding in the Court gayeties and excitements which usually fall to the lot of a Princess, "young, and so fair," none, can question its happiness, for it is a life of duty and devotion.

* * * * *

And now my little biography is finished—"would it were worthier!"—and I must take leave of my illustrious subject, "kissing hands" in imagination, with profound respect. If I back out of the presence, it is not in unrepublican abasement, but because I am loath to turn my eyes away, from the kindly and now familiar face of the good woman, and the good Queen—VICTORIA.

THE END.

Made in the USA
Lexington, KY
01 March 2014